Code of Professional Ethics of the American Institute for CPCU

Code of Professional Ethics of the American Institute for CPCU

Eighth Edition • Third Printing

American Institute for Chartered Property Casualty
Underwriters/Insurance Institute of America
720 Providence Road, Suite 100
Malvern, Pennsylvania 19355-3433

Eighth Edition · Third Printing · November 2008

Library of Congress Control Number: 2007930258

ISBN 978-0-89463-336-2

Printed in Canada

Foreword

The American Institute for Chartered Property Casualty Underwriters and the Insurance Institute of America (the Institutes) are not-for-profit organizations committed to meeting the evolving educational needs of the risk management and insurance community. The Institutes strive to provide current, relevant educational programs in formats that meet the needs of risk management and insurance professionals and the organizations that employ them.

The American Institute for CPCU (AICPCU) was founded in 1942 through a collaborative effort between industry professionals and academics, led by faculty members at The Wharton School of the University of Pennsylvania. In 1953, AICPCU coordinated operations with the Insurance Institute of America (IIA), which was founded in 1909 and remains the oldest continuously functioning national organization offering educational programs for the property-casualty insurance sector.

The Insurance Research Council (IRC), founded in 1977, is a division of AICPCU supported by industry members. This not-for-profit research organization examines public policy issues of interest to property-casualty insurers, insurance customers, and the general public. IRC research reports are distributed widely to insurance-related organizations, public policy authorities, and the media.

The Institutes' new customer- and solution-focused business model allows us to better serve the risk management and insurance communities. Customer-centricity defines our business philosophy and shapes our priorities. The Institutes' innovation arises from our commitment to finding solutions that meet customer needs and deliver results. Our business process is shaped by our commitment to efficiency, strategy, and responsible asset management.

The Institutes believe that professionalism is grounded in education, experience, and ethical behavior. The Chartered Property Casualty Underwriter (CPCU) professional designation offered by the Institutes is designed to provide a broad understanding of the property-casualty insurance industry. Depending on professional needs, CPCU students may select either a commercial or a personal risk management and insurance focus. The CPCU designation is conferred annually by the AICPCU Board of Trustees.

In addition, the Institutes offer designations and certificate programs in a variety of disciplines, including the following:

- Claims
- Commercial underwriting
- Fidelity and surety bonding
- General insurance
- Insurance accounting and finance
- Insurance information technology
- Insurance production and agency management
- Insurance regulation and compliance

- Management
- Marine insurance
- Personal insurance
- Premium auditing
- Quality insurance services
- Reinsurance
- Risk management
- Surplus lines

You can complete a program leading to a designation, take a single course to fill a knowledge gap, or take multiple courses and programs throughout your career. The practical and technical knowledge gained from Institute courses enhances your qualifications and contributes to your professional growth. Most Institute courses carry college credit recommendations from the American Council on Education. A variety of courses qualify for credits toward certain associate, bachelor's, and master's degrees at several prestigious colleges and universities.

Our Knowledge Resources Department, in conjunction with industry experts and members of the academic community, develops our trusted course and program content, including Institute study materials. These materials provide practical career and performance-enhancing knowledge and skills.

We welcome comments from our students and course leaders. Your feedback helps us continue to improve the quality of our study materials.

Peter L. Miller, CPCU
President and CEO
American Institute for CPCU
Insurance Institute of America

Preface

Ethics has always been part of the CPCU movement. The very first CPCU graduating class in 1943 recited the CPCU Charge:

In all of my business dealings and activities I agree to abide by the following rules of professional conduct:

- *I shall strive at all times to ascertain and understand the needs of those whom I serve and act as if their interests were my own; and*

- *I shall do all in my power to maintain and uphold a standard of honor and integrity that will reflect credit on the business in which I am engaged.*

With minor changes, this "Charge," now known as the CPCU Professional Commitment, continues to serve as a pledge that is recited by all CPCUs present at every CPCU conferment ceremony.

The contents of the *Code of Professional Ethics of the American Institute for CPCU* can be summarized as follows:

- Chapter 1 presents an overview of the Code of Professional Ethics of the American Institute for CPCU (Code) and introduces the purpose of the Code, the requirements for earning the CPCU designation, parties affected by the Code, components of the Code, and support for the Code.

- Chapter 2 presents the Canons, Rules, and Guidelines of the Code for ease of reference.

- Chapter 3 provides a commentary on the nine Canons, as well as commentary on the Rules and Guidelines associated with the CPCU Code.

- Chapter 4 describes the disciplinary rules, procedures, and penalties associated with the CPCU Code of Professional Ethics.

- Chapter 5 presents Hypothetical Case Studies and Advisory Opinions of the Institute's Board of Ethical Inquiry.

- Chapter 6 presents the CPCU Society's Code of Professional Ethics.

Appreciation is expressed to Dr. Ronald C. Horn, CPCU, CLU, author and editor of the original Code; and Eric A. Wiening, CPCU, ARM, AU, retired Assistant Vice President and Ethics Counsel of the American Institute for CPCU and coordinating author of the seventh edition.

For more information about the Institutes' programs, please call our Customer Service Department at (800) 644-2101, e-mail us at customerservice@cpcuiia.org, or visit our Web site at www.aicpcu.org.

Lowell S. Young

Contents

Chapter 1

Overview of the Code of Professional Ethics

This chapter presents an overview of the Code of Professional Ethics of the American Institute for Chartered Property Casualty Underwriters (the Code), its purpose, the related requirements for earning the Chartered Property Casualty Underwriter (CPCU) designation, the parties it affects, and its components.

The Code was introduced in 1976. Therefore, all who became CPCUs in 1976 or after are bound by it. Most who received the CPCU designation before 1976 signed a statement agreeing to be bound by the Code.

PURPOSE OF THE CODE OF PROFESSIONAL ETHICS

The goals described in the Code's Canons direct all CPCUs and CPCU candidates to always perform their professional activities ethically. The minimum standards of conduct that the Code's Rules describe support the integrity of the CPCU designation. All CPCUs are obligated to meet these minimum standards. Failure to do so may subject a CPCU—or a CPCU candidate—to disciplinary measures.

The Code is included among CPCU study materials to ensure that all CPCUs understand their ethical obligations. The Code also includes provisions for its orderly enforcement.

Only the American Institute is authorized to confer the CPCU designation. The American Institute confers the CPCU designation upon individuals who have met the three requirements—education, experience, and ethics—established by its Board of Trustees.

The Board of Trustees also can revoke the designation or otherwise discipline CPCUs who violate one or more Rules of the Code. Revocation of the CPCU designation is the ultimate disciplinary action under the Code. Lesser sanctions, such as a reprimand, may also be imposed, depending on the severity of the offense.

REQUIREMENTS FOR EARNING THE CPCU DESIGNATION

To earn the CPCU designation, candidates must meet the following education, experience, and ethics requirements:

Education Requirement

The American Institute publishes specific details of its education requirement, which is periodically modified, in other materials. The education requirement is typically met by passing an exam in each of eight courses (five foundation courses in addition to three courses from either the commercial or personal concentration).

The CPCU curriculum includes the following five foundation courses:

1. CPCU 510—Foundations of Risk Management, Insurance, and Professionalism
2. CPCU 520—Insurance Operations, Regulation, and Statutory Accounting
3. CPCU 530—The Legal Environment of Insurance
4. CPCU 540—Finance for Risk Management and Insurance Professionals
5. CPCU 560—Financial Services Institutions

The commercial concentration courses include the following:

- CPCU 551—Commercial Property Risk Management and Insurance
- CPCU 552—Commercial Liability Risk Management and Insurance
- CPCU 553—Survey of Personal Risk Management, Insurance, and Financial Planning

The personal concentration courses include the following:

- CPCU 555—Personal Risk Management and Property-Liability Insurance
- CPCU 556—Personal Financial Planning
- CPCU 557—Survey of Commercial Risk Management and Insurance

Since the CPCU program's introduction in 1942, its education requirement has focused on insurance and risk management but also has included general business topics that relate to insurance and risk management. This broad education requirement ensures that CPCUs are knowledgeable about not only insurance and risk but also the business environment.

Experience Requirement

The American Institute requires each CPCU candidate to meet a three-year experience requirement before obtaining the designation. During the five-year period immediately preceding the conferment of the CPCU designation, a candidate must have been engaged in acceptable insurance activities for any thirty-six-month period for a minimum of seventeen and a half hours per week. Acceptable insurance activities are broadly interpreted and include the following:

- Insurance sales and related account services
- Insurance activities and services such as claim settlement, inspection, loss control, premium auditing, ratemaking, rating, reinsurance, and underwriting
- Support functions such as accounting, clerical, education and training, information systems, investment services, legal services, and personnel administration, if performed for a firm or department primarily engaged in insurance
- Job roles such as attorney, certified public accountant, college teacher, consultant, or risk manager; or employee of a regulatory authority, salvage company, trade association, trade press, or a similar organization working with or as a part of the insurance industry

A candidate who meets all requirements except the experience requirement becomes a CPCU after he or she has met the experience requirement.

Ethics Requirement

Matriculation is the process of registering as a CPCU candidate. By matriculating, a CPCU candidate declares that he or she intends to become a CPCU and agrees to adhere to the American Institute's requirements. In signing a matriculation form, a candidate also agrees to the following statement:

> I agree that as a condition of the acceptance of my application and of my continued good standing as a CPCU candidate and as the holder of the CPCU designation, I shall abide by the Code of Professional Ethics of the American Institute for Chartered Property Casualty Underwriters.

The American Institute may, at its discretion, ask for references after receiving the matriculation form from the student and again when the student registers for his or her final CPCU exam.

Matriculation
The process of registering as a CPCU candidate.

PARTIES AFFECTED BY THE CODE

The Code applies to applicants, candidates, designees, and CPCUs, defined as follows:

- An **applicant** is a CPCU student who has submitted a matriculation form that has not yet been approved. In rare cases, an applicant may be rejected and not become a candidate.
- A **candidate** is a CPCU student whose matriculation application has been approved.
- A **designee** is a person who has earned the CPCU designation, regardless of whether he or she has officially become a CPCU. Those who have met all requirements but are waiting for notification of the date on which they will become CPCUs are referred to as designees; those currently receiving the CPCU designation are also considered designees.

Applicant
A CPCU student who has submitted a matriculation form that has not yet been approved.

Candidate
A CPCU student whose matriculation application has been approved.

Designee
A person who has earned the CPCU designation, regardless of whether he or she has officially become a CPCU.

CPCU
A person who currently holds the CPCU designation.

- A **CPCU** is a person who currently holds the CPCU designation. If someone's designation is revoked or suspended, that person is no longer a CPCU and is no longer permitted to use the CPCU designation.

For the purposes of this discussion, designees or those waiting for conferment may also be referred to as CPCUs.

Applicants

A person may matriculate as a CPCU candidate at any time, even without registering for a CPCU exam. CPCU candidates are encouraged to matriculate when they begin the CPCU program, but they are not required to do so until they have satisfied the educational requirements.

The matriculation form can identify an applicant whose eligibility as a CPCU candidate may raise ethical concerns. Such applicants are urged to matriculate as soon as possible in order to allow any potential issues of concern to be resolved.

In cases involving serious ethical issues, a student's matriculation application is reviewed by Ethics Counsel, which may request additional information before accepting or rejecting the application. In some instances, an applicant's eligibility to become a candidate and take further CPCU exams may be suspended temporarily or indefinitely.

CPCU Candidates

All CPCU candidates are bound by the Code when they matriculate and for as long as they remain candidates. Because CPCU candidacy has no term limits, a matriculated CPCU student remains a candidate until conferment of the designation, unless his or her conferment has been deferred or candidacy has been suspended or revoked.

CPCUs

All CPCUs, with the previously discussed exceptions, are bound by the Code. The small number of CPCUs who received their designations before 1976 and chose not to be bound by the Code are not subject to discipline or penalties under the Code. In one case in which the American Institute lacked jurisdiction over a pre-1976 CPCU, the CPCU Society expelled the CPCU for unethical conduct. The CPCU Society has its own separate Code of Ethics and has the right to suspend or revoke a person's Society membership even if he or she retains the CPCU designation.

COMPONENTS OF THE CODE

The Code includes Canons, Rules, and Guidelines. Hypothetical Case Studies demonstrate how the Code may be applied in particular situations. Advisory Opinions are useful for interpreting the various Code provisions. The Code also includes Disciplinary Rules, Procedures, and Penalties that explain the process by which it is administered and enforced.

Canons, Rules, and Guidelines

The Canons, Rules, and Guidelines serve distinct functions:

- The **Canons** are broad aspirational goals of CPCU conduct.
- The **Rules** are specific, enforceable standards that prescribe the minimum levels of required professional CPCU conduct. They are enforceable because sanctions may be imposed on any CPCU or candidate found guilty of a Rule violation.
- **Guidelines** are instructions that are enforceable when they are specifically part of a Rule. The Guidelines help candidates and CPCUs interpret other Code provisions, especially the Rules. Other Guidelines are provided to help candidates and CPCUs interpret other Code provisions. The enforceable Guidelines refer to the use of the CPCU designation and the CPCU key logo. For example, they explain when it is appropriate to use the letters "CPCU" and where it is appropriate to display the CPCU key logo.

The Canons in the Code establish standards of professional conduct. They also express the general concepts and principles from which the more specific Rules are derived.

Each of the Canons is followed by one or more related Rules. Unlike the Canons, the Rules are specific mandatory, enforceable standards. The Rules prescribe the absolute minimum level of ethical conduct required of every CPCU, regardless of occupational position. Any individual subject to the Code who violates a Rule faces the possibility of disciplinary action. Only the Rules are enforceable. In the absence of a Rule violation, violations of Canons and/or Guidelines do not constitute sufficient grounds for disciplinary action.

The Rules are followed by Guidelines related to the Rules. Guidelines assist CPCUs and CPCU candidates in interpreting the various Code provisions, understanding their rationale, and applying them to frequently encountered situations that require ethical judgment. Individuals subject to the Code are exposed to the possibility of disciplinary action for violations of any Guidelines that have been incorporated by reference into the Rules.

Canons
Broad aspirational goals of CPCU conduct.

Rules
Specific, enforceable standards that prescribe the minimum levels of required professional CPCU conduct.

Guidelines
Instructions that are enforceable when they are specifically part of a Rule.

Hypothetical Case Studies (HCSs)

Hypothetical Case Studies (HCSs) pose a variety of ethical questions and issues to which the Code may be applied. They also indicate how the Code's drafters envisioned its application. The commentary that accompanies the Code lists the applicable HCSs and related Rules for each Canon.

Advisory Opinions

Advisory Opinion
A written interpretation of the CPCU Code of Professional Ethics provided by the Board of Ethical Inquiry.

Board of Ethical Inquiry (BEI)
An eight-member board, chaired by the Ethics Counsel, responsible for implementing, establishing, and approving CPCU ethics policy.

Ethics Counsel
The chair of the Board of Ethical Inquiry (BEI) who receives written complaints of ethical violations, investigates the complaints and presents the facts to the BEI for consideration, and communicates BEI recommendations to the Ethics Policy Committee of the Board of Trustees of the American Institute and delivers the verdicts.

CPCUs and CPCU candidates are strongly encouraged to request Advisory Opinions from the American Institute whenever substantial questions of interpretation arise. An **Advisory Opinion** is a written interpretation of the CPCU Code of Professional Ethics provided by the Board of Ethical Inquiry (BEI). The **Board of Ethical Inquiry** is an eight-member board, chaired by the Ethics Counsel, responsible for implementing, establishing, and approving CPCU ethics policy.

Advisory opinions may be either unpublished or published. Unpublished Advisory Opinions are informal Advisory Opinions issued by the BEI intended solely for the individuals to whom they are issued. Published Advisory Opinions are formal Advisory Opinions issued by the BEI intended for all persons subject to the Code.

Ethics Counsel is the chair of the BEI who receives written complaints of ethical violations, investigates the complaints and presents the facts to the BEI for consideration, and communicates BEI recommendations to the Ethics Policy Committee of the Board of Trustees of the American Institute and delivers the verdicts.

Unpublished Advisory Opinions may lead to a published Advisory Opinion. For example, informal, unpublished Advisory Opinions were issued in response to questions regarding the appropriate use of the CPCU key logo and designation on Web pages. After discussion, the BEI unanimously approved an Advisory Opinion published in the *CPCU Journal* in late 1998. This Advisory Opinion appears in the discussion of Canon 8.

Disciplinary Rules, Procedures, and Penalties

The right to use the CPCU designation is a privilege granted by the Board of Trustees and conditioned on full compliance with the Rules of Professional Conduct. The Board of Trustees reserves the power to suspend or revoke the privilege or approve other penalties recommended by the BEI. Disciplinary penalties are imposed as warranted by the severity of the offense and its attendant circumstances. All disciplinary actions are undertaken in accordance with published procedures and penalties designed to ensure the proper enforcement of the Rules within the framework of due process and equal protection of the laws.

The Disciplinary Rules, Procedures, and Penalties describe the procedures to be followed in response to possible Rule violations and also describe possible sanctions.

Procedures

Procedural information is available as a reference to CPCUs or candidates who become subject to discipline under the Code. The procedural information is also relevant to those who enforce the Code and to CPCUs and others who may want to lodge a formal complaint under the Code.

Brief Summary of the Disciplinary Process

All complaints alleging violation of the Code should be submitted in writing to the American Institute's Ethics Counsel:

> Ethics Counsel, American Institute for CPCU, 720 Providence Road, Suite 100, Malvern, PA 19355-3433, USA. (EthicsCounsel@cpcuiia.org)

If the American Institute has jurisdiction and the claim has sufficient merit, a formal investigation is initiated and a copy of the complaint provided to the person or persons against whom the complaint is lodged, who may then respond.

The specific nature of any investigation depends on the circumstances of the complaint. Ultimately, a three-member hearing panel of the BEI makes a recommendation to the entire BEI. The BEI recommendation, in turn, is considered by the **Ethics Policy Committee** of the American Institute's Board of Trustees, which is a committee of the Board of Trustees of the American Institute that reviews matters of policy relating to American Institute ethics activities and promulgates the specific disciplinary procedures and penalties to be used in enforcing the Code. All revocations and suspensions of the privilege to use the CPCU designation are reported in writing to the American Institute's Board of Trustees.

Ethics Policy Committee
A committee of the Board of Trustees of the American Institute that reviews matters of policy relating to American Institute ethics activities and promulgates the specific disciplinary procedures and penalties to be used in enforcing the Code.

Parties bringing a complaint are sometimes frustrated by the amount of time that elapses before its resolution. However, the process described in the Disciplinary Rules, Procedures, and Penalties ensures fairness to persons who are the subject of a complaint.

As discussed in connection with Canon 3, some Rules violations involving criminal conviction may subject a CPCU or candidate to automatic suspension without the procedural steps that may otherwise be involved, because the conviction itself is objective evidence of a Rule violation.

Sanctions and Penalties Under the Code

The sanctions that may be applied to CPCU applicants and candidates differ from those applicable to CPCUs.

CPCU Applicants and Candidates. Applicant-related complaints typically involve past activities of a questionable nature that fall under the Rules of Canons 3 and 4. Most CPCU candidate-related complaints involve cheating on a CPCU exam, a violation of the Rules under Canon 3.

Both applicants and candidates may be penalized by being denied admission to further CPCU exams, either indefinitely or for a specified time period. The BEI may also withhold awarding the CPCU designation, pending receipt of convincing proof of a candidate's complete rehabilitation. Candidates may also be subject to admonition, reprimand, or censure, depending on the nature and severity of the offense.

A CPCU candidate is immediately suspended from further participation in the CPCU program if convicted—by verdict, guilty plea, or plea of nolo contendere—of any crime that violates the Rules of Professional Conduct. This suspension will last indefinitely, or until the BEI has been convinced that the person is again fit to use the designation.

Only certain crimes violate the Rules. The distinctions are discussed in connection with Rule R3.3.

CPCUs. The BEI may impose any of the following five sanctions on a CPCU who is subject to the Code and found guilty of a Rules violation:

1. Private admonition, including a request to cease and desist
2. Reprimand (informal rebuke given limited publication)
3. Censure (formal rebuke given wide publication)
4. Suspension of the privilege to use the designation, indefinitely or for a specific time period
5. Revocation of the designation

The terms "limited publication" and "wide publication" are not defined in the Code. The nature of the publication is decided on a case-by-case basis. If the violation is not serious, publication may be limited to simply informing the parties to the complaint of the decision. In other, more serious cases, the action is published in the *CPCU News*, a periodical sent to all current members of the CPCU Society. The CPCU is named, but the nature of the charge may not be described.

Suspension implies the possibility that the designee may be permitted to use the CPCU designation in the future. A CPCU whose designation has been revoked may also apply for reinstatement.

In most circumstances, a CPCU may be disciplined only after an investigation leading to a vote by the BEI. A CPCU's designation is immediately suspended if the CPCU is convicted, by verdict, guilty plea, or plea of nolo contendere, of any crime that violates the Rules of Professional Conduct. This suspension lasts indefinitely, or until the BEI has been convinced that the person is again fit to use the designation.

The Canons, Rules, and Guidelines of the Code of Professional Ethics

CHAPTER 2

CANON 1

CPCUs should endeavor at all times to place the public interest above their own.

Rules of Professional Conduct

R1.1   A CPCU has a duty to understand and abide by all Rules of conduct prescribed in the Code of Professional Ethics (the Code).

R1.2   A CPCU shall not advocate, sanction, participate in, cause to be accomplished, otherwise carry out through another, or condone any act the CPCU is prohibited from performing by the Rules of the Code.

Guidelines for Professional Conduct

G1.1   By stipulating that CPCUs should endeavor at all times to place the public interest above their own, Canon 1 serves as the fundamental goal of the entire Code. The other Code standards define the "public interest" (and hence the ethical obligations of CPCUs) more specifically.

CPCUs can place the public interest above their own by understanding and obeying all the Rules in the Code (as specified in R1.1 and R1.2) and then, beyond the expected minimums, by striving to meet the standards expressed in the Canons and the Guidelines. A formal commitment to altruism is probably the single most important characteristic that defines professional behavior.

G1.2   A CPCU should avoid even the appearance of impropriety when performing his or her professional duties and should act in a manner that ultimately will best serve his or her own professional interests. This Guideline, followed in conjunction with the other provisions of the Code, should pose no insurmountable problems of priority in most situations because a CPCU's best long-term professional interests ordinarily do not conflict either with the public interest or with other specific interests. However, potential conflicts of interest may arise, or may appear to arise, because many CPCUs simultaneously must balance multiple professional interests with their personal interests and the best interests of the general public. For example, a CPCU employed by an insurer may serve his or her immediate superior, the corporation, the stockholders, the policyholders, agents, and industry associations. An agent may serve his or her clients; two or more insurers; and his or her business partners, stockholders, or associates.

Strict compliance with all the Rules of the Code, including R1.2, should enable a CPCU to resolve such potential conflicts of interest. However, when a person subject to the Code is uncertain about the ethical propriety of a specific activity or type of conduct, he or she should refrain from engaging in the questionable activity or conduct until the matter has been clarified. Any CPCU or CPCU candidate who needs assistance in interpreting the Code is encouraged to request an advisory opinion from the American Institute's Board of Ethical Inquiry (BEI).

G1.3   The ethical obligation to place the public interest above personal interests or financial gain extends to every CPCU, regardless of whether the CPCU's occupational position requires direct contact with actual or prospective insurance consumers.

G1.4   The Guidelines do not imply that insurance purchasers should be given preferential treatment over insurance claimants because the needs and best interests of insurance purchasers are in fact served only when all insurance claimants, including third-party liability claimants, are accorded prompt, equitable, and otherwise fair treatment.

CANON 2

CPCUs should seek continually to maintain and improve their professional knowledge, skills, and competence.

Rules of Professional Conduct

R2.1   A CPCU shall keep informed on technical matters that are essential to the maintenance of the CPCU's professional competence in insurance, risk management, or related fields.

Guidelines for Professional Conduct

G2.1   Though knowledge and skills alone do not ensure that an individual will adhere to high ethical standards, they are requisites to the high levels of competence and performance expected of all professionals. This is especially true for practitioners in a business such as insurance, which is characterized not only by its existing complexities but also by rapid changes in the business and in the legal, economic, and social environments in which it operates. If an individual purports to be a professional and yet does not maintain high levels of competence and performance, he or she engages in unethical conduct. Therefore, every CPCU has an ethical obligation to engage actively and continuously in appropriate educational activities.

G2.2   At a minimum, as specified in Rule R2.1, "A CPCU shall keep informed on technical matters that are essential to the maintenance of his or her professional competence in insurance, risk management, or related fields." Because CPCUs serve as agents, brokers, underwriters, claim representatives, actuaries, risk managers, regulators, company executives, and specialists in a wide variety of insurance-related fields, the Rule does not attempt to prescribe the specific technical matters that are essential to the maintenance of professional competence in each of the numerous specialties. Instead, a CPCU must decide, in the light of his or her occupational position, the content and form of continuing education that will satisfy R2.1.

G2.3   Many professions have established mandatory continuing education requirements that impose severe penalties on members who do not periodically certify that they have met at least one of the specified continuing education options. The trustees of the American Institute have no plans to require CPCUs to certify periodically that they have met the obligations under Rule R2.1. However, the maintenance of professional competence is considered a minimum obligation of every CPCU. The BEI will investigate alleged violations of Rule R2.1 and may impose warranted penalties on violators. Furthermore, if a CPCU is accused of violating any other Rule, the Board may, at its discretion, require the accused to furnish evidence of compliance with Rule R2.1.

G2.4   Beyond the minimum continuing education requirements referred to in Rule R2.1, all CPCUs are urged to engage in additional pursuits that will meet the aspirational goal, under Canon 2, of improving their professional knowledge, skills, and competence.

For example, the BEI suggests that every CPCU qualify for recognition under the Continuing Professional Development (CPD) program, which is jointly sponsored by the American Institute and the CPCU Society.

The CPD program recognizes those who have met specific criteria. The requirements of the CPD program, which are occasionally revised, are automatically distributed to members of the CPCU Society and are available to others on request. Points are assigned to various activities. Current criteria include the following:

- Passing an exam or a course in a respected insurance or business-related program

- Passing a college or university course in insurance, risk management, or a business-related subject

- Teaching a course in insurance, risk management, or a business-related subject

- Authoring or coauthoring an article accepted for publication in the *CPCU e-Journal* or similar business publication, a CPCU Society section newsletter, or a textbook

- Conducting a research project

- Serving as an officer, a director, a committee chair, or a committee member of a national insurance organization or local CPCU chapter

- Serving as a class coordinator for a CPCU chapter or another course-sponsoring organization

- Serving on a state insurance advisory committee

- Grading CPCU or Insurance Institute of America (IIA) exams

- Serving on exam-development committees for CPCU, IIA, state licensing, or other examination programs

- Attending the CPCU Annual Meeting and Seminars or the annual meetings of other national insurance organizations

- Attending educational meetings, seminars, videoconferences, or workshops sponsored by the CPCU Society or others

- Attending meetings of CPCU chapters or other insurance organizations that include a speaker or an educational program

- Meeting state continuing education requirements for licensing

- Being an expert witness

- Serving as a personal sponsor for CPCU and IIA students

CANON 3

CPCUs should obey all laws and regulations, and should avoid any conduct or activity that would cause unjust harm to others.

Rules of Professional Conduct

R3.1   In the conduct of business or professional activities, a CPCU shall not engage in any act or omission of a dishonest, deceitful, or fraudulent nature.

R3.2   A CPCU shall not allow the pursuit of financial gain or other personal benefit to interfere with the exercise of sound professional judgment and skills.

R3.3   A CPCU shall not violate any law or regulation relating to professional activities or commit any felony.

Guidelines for Professional Conduct

G3.1   A CPCU should neither misrepresent nor conceal a fact or information that is material to determining the suitability, efficacy, scope, or limitations of an insurance contract or a surety bond. Nor should a CPCU materially misrepresent or conceal the financial condition, or the quality of services, of any insurer or reinsurer. The extent to which a CPCU should volunteer information and facts must necessarily be left to sound professional judgment. This Guideline illustrates the kinds of acts and omissions that can be "dishonest, deceitful, or fraudulent," in violation of Rule R3.1, and that normally "would cause unjust harm to others," thus violating the spirit of Canon 3.

G3.2   A CPCU should not, to the detriment of the insuring public, engage in any business practice or activity designed to restrict fair competition. However, this Guideline does not prohibit a CPCU's participation in a legally enforceable covenant not to compete, or in a similar activity specifically sanctioned or required by law.

G3.3   When performing his or her occupational function, a CPCU should not, at the expense of the uninformed, deliberately achieve or seek to achieve financial gain for the CPCU or the CPCU's employer that is unconscionable relative to the customary gains for the quantity and quality of services actually rendered.

Generally, no CPCU should seek or accept compensation that is neither for nor commensurate with professional services actually rendered or to be rendered. Nor should any CPCU seek or accept compensation under any other terms, conditions, or circumstances that would violate any Canon, Rule, or Guideline in this Code. However, nothing in this Guideline prohibits seeking or accepting gifts from family or personal friends, income from investments, or income from any other activity that would neither prevent nor inherently impair the free and complete exercise of the CPCU's sound professional judgment and skills nor otherwise violate the Code.

A CPCU should not perform professional services under terms, conditions, or circumstances that would prevent or inherently impair the free and complete exercise of the CPCU's sound professional judgment and skills. This Guideline does not prohibit a CPCU from being compensated under the terms of a legally acceptable commission arrangement, because such an arrangement does not prevent or inherently impair the CPCU's professional judgment and skills. But it does serve to remind a CPCU so compensated of his or her ethical obligation to avoid any recommendation to a consumer of the CPCU's services that would increase the CPCU's compensation, unless such recommendation clearly meets the consumer's legitimate needs and best interests. The Guideline also serves to remind every CPCU, regardless of his or her basis of compensation, of the ethical obligation to render fully such services as are contemplated and rightfully owed under the terms of the applicable compensation arrangement.

G3.4   While the American Institute's standards of ethical conduct are not limited to the duties and obligations imposed upon CPCUs by the laws and regulations governing the conduct of all insurance practitioners, obedience to and respect for law and regulatory authority are absolute minimum standards of professional conduct. The potential consequences of violating this admonition extend beyond those that may fall upon the violator, because one CPCU's violation of laws or regulations may discredit the CPCU designation itself.

A CPCU is obligated to keep informed of every law and regulation governing or otherwise pertaining to his or her business activities and, when necessary, should seek interpretive assistance from the appropriate regulatory officials and/or retain the services of competent legal counsel. If a CPCU doubts the legality of a particular kind of business conduct or activity, he or she should refrain from such conduct or activity. A CPCU may not plead lack of knowledge as a defense for improper conduct under Rule R3.3 unless he or she can demonstrate that a reasonable, good-faith effort was made to obtain such knowledge, and it was not available.

CANON 4

CPCUs should be diligent in the performance of their occupational duties and should continually strive to improve the functioning of the insurance mechanism.

Rules of Professional Conduct

R4.1   A CPCU shall competently and consistently discharge his or her occupational duties.

R4.2   A CPCU shall support efforts to effect improvements in claim settlement, contract design, investment, marketing, pricing, reinsurance, safety engineering, underwriting, and other insurance operations that will both benefit the public and improve the overall efficiency with which the insurance mechanism functions.

Guidelines for Professional Conduct

G4.1   The public expects both competence and diligence from profession-als. Thus, to complement Rule R2.1, which obligates a CPCU to maintain professional competence by keeping informed, Rule R4.1 stipulates that "a CPCU shall competently and consistently discharge his or her occupational duties."

Although the BEI believes that all professionals, including CPCUs, should perform diligently, it will not intervene or arbitrate between the parties in an employment, or a contractual, relationship or a civil dispute. Nor are the American Institute's disciplinary procedures a substitute for legal and other remedies available to such parties. In the event of an alleged violation of Rule R4.1, therefore, the Board will hear the case only after all other remedies have been exhausted, and it generally will take disciplinary action only in circumstances in which a proven violation has caused unjust harm to another person and the violation brings substantial discredit upon the CPCU designation; or it would otherwise be in the public interest to take disciplinary action under the Code.

G4.2   In addition to competently and consistently discharging his or her own occupational duties, a CPCU is obligated by Rule R4.2 "to support efforts to effect such improvements [in insurer functions and operations] that will both benefit the public and improve the overall efficiency with which the insurance mechanism functions." This emphasizes that it is possible to effect improvements in insurer efficiency and profitability in a manner contrary to the public inter-est. It is sometimes difficult to determine whether a proposed change will both improve overall efficiency and benefit the public, but the CPCU's ethical obligation, consistent with the theme expressed in Canon 1, is to support efforts to effect such improvements. The kinds of efforts that satisfy both criteria, and that the Board believes a CPCU should support, are illustrated in the following Guidelines:

G4.3   A CPCU should assist in improving the language, suitability, adaptability, and general efficacy of insurance contracts and surety bonds.

G4.4   A CPCU should assist in ensuring protection and security for the public, and in maintaining and improving the integrity of the insurance institution, by helping to preserve and improve the financial strength of all private insurers.

G4.5   A CPCU should assist in providing an adequate supply of insurance and surety bonds to meet public demands and needs.

G4.6   A CPCU should assist in minimizing the cost to the public of insurance and suretyship, without compromising the quality of benefits or services provided, by helping to improve the operational efficiency of insurers and their representatives by contributing to the solution of economic, legal, political, and other social problems that demonstrably increase the cost of insurance and suretyship without enhancing quality or otherwise improving public well-being. Examples of such problems include inflation, unemployment, crime, inequities and inefficiencies in the legal system, inequities and inefficiencies in the healthcare delivery system, floods, and other natural catastrophes. The availability of insurance alone will not solve such problems. However, a CPCU should not neglect his or her personal duty to become actively involved in the search for underlying causes of, and long-term solutions to, such problems.

G4.7   Because of a CPCU's professional capabilities and knowledge of the magnitude of human and dollar losses suffered annually, he or she should assume an especially active role in private and public loss-prevention and loss-reduction efforts. A CPCU should do the utmost to preserve human life; maintain and improve the physical and mental health of all human beings; and prevent the damage, destruction, and abstraction of property.

G4.8   A CPCU should participate in and support research that helps to improve the private insurance mechanism and research that helps reduce losses of life, health, or property.

G4.9   The ethical obligation to strive for improvement in the functioning of the private insurance mechanism does not bar a CPCU from serving in the public sector, nor does it bar a CPCU, as an individual citizen, from supporting a governmental role in providing economic security for the citizenry. But a CPCU should be mindful of the restriction imposed by R8.4, and should avoid even the appearance of speaking on behalf of the American Institute, especially on political matters.

CANON 5

CPCUs should assist in maintaining and raising professional standards in the insurance business.

Rules of Professional Conduct

R5.1   A CPCU shall support personnel policies and practices that attract qualified individuals to the insurance business, provide them with ample and equal opportunities for advancement, and encourage them to aspire to the highest levels of professional competence and achievement.

R5.2   A CPCU shall encourage and assist qualified individuals who wish to pursue CPCU or other studies that will enhance their professional competence.

R5.3   A CPCU shall support the development, improvement, and enforcement of laws, regulations, and codes that will foster competence and ethical conduct on the part of all insurance practitioners and benefit the public.

R5.4   A CPCU shall not withhold information or assistance officially requested by appropriate regulatory authorities who are investigating or prosecuting any alleged violation of laws or regulations.

Guidelines for Professional Conduct

G5.1   A CPCU should assist in raising professional standards in the insurance business. Minimally, every CPCU should conduct his or her business activities in a manner that will inspire other practitioners to do likewise.

G5.2   Both the insuring public and the insurance industry will benefit from continued growth in the number of insurance practitioners who achieve a high level of professional attainment. Thus, Rule R5.2 stipulates that "A CPCU shall encourage and assist qualified individuals who wish to pursue CPCU or other studies that will enhance their professional competence."

A CPCU should share with all other insurance practitioners, as well as fellow CPCUs, the benefits of his or her professional attainments. A CPCU's conduct should be guided by a spirit of altruistic concern for the public interest. The public interest is best served when all insurance practitioners are well-informed.

A CPCU should support and participate in educational activities that assist other practitioners in their professional development. Examples of such activities include seminars, lectures, research projects, teaching, preparation of educational materials for training programs, and preparation of professional articles for publication. In writing or speaking publicly as a CPCU, however, the CPCU should maintain the dignity and high professional standards appropriate to the designation.

This Guideline does not obligate a CPCU to divulge trade secrets or other information that would put him or her at a competitive disadvantage. Instead, it serves as a reminder that a CPCU should play a role in the development of the insurance field by sharing knowledge with other practitioners and students.

CANON 6

CPCUs should strive to establish and maintain dignified and honorable relationships with those whom they serve, with fellow insurance practitioners, and with members of other professions.

Rules of Professional Conduct

R6.1   A CPCU shall keep informed on the legal limitations imposed on the scope of his or her professional duties.

R6.2   A CPCU shall not disclose any confidential information entrusted to, or obtained by, the CPCU in the course of his or her business or professional activities, unless a disclosure of such information is required by law or is made to a person who necessarily must have the information in order to discharge occupational or professional duties.

R6.3   In rendering or proposing to render professional services for others, a CPCU shall not knowingly misrepresent or conceal any limitations on his or her ability to provide the quantity or quality of professional services the circumstances require.

Guidelines for Professional Conduct

G6.1   By exhibiting high levels of professional competence and ethical conduct, a CPCU should constantly strive to merit the confidence and respect of those whom he or she serves, fellow practitioners, and members of other professions.

G6.2   A CPCU should strive to establish and maintain dignified and honorable relationships with competitors, as well as with fellow practitioners.

G6.3   A CPCU should strive to establish and maintain dignified and honorable relationships with members of other professions, including but not limited to law, medicine, and accounting. The insurance industry relies heavily on the expertise and cooperation of such professionals in fulfilling its obligation to deliver insurance benefits promptly and otherwise render high-quality insurance service to the public.

G6.4   Like other professionals, a CPCU should maintain the knowledge and skills necessary to exercise independent judgment in the performance of his or her professional services. However, a CPCU should also be mindful of his or her personal limitations. Therefore, a CPCU should seek the counsel of other professionals, not only at the request of those whom he or she may serve but also on the CPCU's own initiative, particularly in doubtful or difficult situations or when the quality of professional service may otherwise be enhanced by such consultation.

G6.5   A CPCU is obligated to keep fully informed on any and all legal limitations imposed on the scope of his or her professional activities. A CPCU should always exercise caution to avoid engaging in, or giving the appearance of engaging in, the unauthorized practice of law. However, a CPCU who is otherwise qualified by virtue of his or her admission to the bar may practice law.

G6.6   Beyond the obligations under Rule R6.2, a CPCU should exercise caution and sound judgment in dealing with any confidential or privileged information.

CANON 7

CPCUs should assist in improving the public understanding of insurance and risk management.

Rules of Professional Conduct

R7.1   A CPCU shall support efforts to provide members of the public with objective information concerning their risk management and insurance needs and the products, services, and techniques available to meet their needs.

R7.2   A CPCU shall not misrepresent the benefits, costs, or limitations of any risk management technique or any product or service of an insurer.

Guidelines for Professional Conduct

G7.1   Fulfillment of all the public's insurance needs would appreciably enhance the economic and social well-being of society. But the public's insurance needs can be fully met only if every citizen recognizes his or her insurance needs and appreciates the importance of seeking competent and ethical assistance in analyzing and meeting them. This requires the combined efforts of all knowledgeable insurance professionals. Accordingly, every CPCU should assist in every practical manner to improve the public understanding of insurance and risk management, even if the CPCU does not specialize in insurance education, marketing, claim settlement, safety engineering, advertising, or other professional activities that provide frequent opportunities to communicate directly to the public.

G7.2   A CPCU should keep abreast of legislation, changing conditions, and/or other developments that may affect the insuring public and should assist in keeping the public informed of such.

G7.3   In order to contribute to a better public understanding of insurance and risk management, every CPCU should maintain and improve his or her knowledge and communication skills. However, no CPCU should hesitate to admit that he or she does not know the answer to a question. Nor should a CPCU attempt to answer such a question if it is outside the realm of his or her professional competence, authority, or proper function.

G7.4   A CPCU should neither engage in nor condone deceptive advertising or business practices that significantly mislead the public or otherwise contribute to the widespread misunderstanding or misuse of insurance. All CPCU communication with the public should provide objective and factual information.

G7.5   The public should recognize its overall risk management needs and the extent to which insurance can and cannot meet them. For example, a CPCU should seize opportunities to stress the importance of loss prevention and reduction in any well-conceived risk management program.

G7.6   Rule R7.1 stipulates that "A CPCU shall support efforts to provide members of the public with objective information concerning their risk management and insurance needs and the products, services, and techniques available to meet their needs." However, neither the Rules nor the Guidelines require a CPCU to support lobbying efforts or proposed legislation or to take positions on controversial issues. Nor do any of the Code standards prohibit a CPCU from engaging in such activities in his or her own name and as an individual. A CPCU who elects to engage in such activities should take great care to avoid violating Rule R8.4.

CANON 8

CPCUs should honor the integrity of the CPCU designation and respect the limitations placed on its use.

Rules of Professional Conduct

R8.1   A CPCU shall use the CPCU designation and the CPCU key only in accordance with the relevant Guidelines promulgated by the American Institute.

R8.2   A CPCU shall not attribute to the mere possession of the designation depth or scope of knowledge, skills, and professional capabilities greater than those demonstrated by successful completion of the CPCU program.

R8.3   A CPCU shall not make unfair comparisons between a person who holds the CPCU designation and one who does not.

R8.4   A CPCU shall not write, speak, or act in a way that leads another to reasonably believe the CPCU is officially representing the American Institute, unless the CPCU has been authorized to do so by the American Institute.

Guidelines for Professional Conduct

G8.1   Rule R8.1 of the Code of Professional Ethics stipulates that "A CPCU shall use the CPCU designation and the CPCU key only in accordance with the relevant Guidelines promulgated by the American Institute." These Guidelines, which define and impose restrictions upon the privilege to use the CPCU designation and key, are set forth subsequently. They are designed to prevent undignified commercialization of the designation, unfair comparison with able and well-established insurance practitioners who do not hold the designation, and other unethical practices inconsistent with the professional concepts that the CPCU represents. Specifically, every CPCU has an ethical obligation to comply with the following minimum standards:

a.   The designation Chartered Property Casualty Underwriter, the initials CPCU, and the CPCU key may be used only in a dignified and professional manner, according to the following provisions:

1.   The designation or initials may be used after the holder's name on business cards, stationery, office advertising, signed articles, business and professional listings, and telephone listings, except where such use would conflict with the provisions of subparagraph a.3.

2. The CPCU key (actual size or reduced, but not enlarged) may be imprinted only on business cards and stationery used exclusively by CPCUs. Copies of the CPCU key suitable for reproduction are available from the American Institute.

3. The designation itself, the initials CPCU, and the CPCU key are not to be used as part of a firm, partnership, or corporate name, trademark, or logo, or affixed to any object, product, or property, for any purpose whatsoever, except by the American Institute.

b. The designation Chartered Property Casualty Underwriter, the initials CPCU, and the CPCU key may be used to announce the conferment of the designation.

1. News releases prepared by the American Institute are made available to all new CPCU designees. Only these approved releases, with the addition of personal biographical information, may be used by individual CPCU designees in preparing material for the business and community press.

2. The American Institute encourages employers of new designees to publish in company publications articles congratulating the new designees. The American Institute's official listing of new designees, published at the time of the conferment ceremony, should be used to verify the names of new designees. Copies of the CPCU key are available from the American Institute for reproduction in such articles.

3. The American Institute encourages the use of dignified advertisements congratulating new designees on earning the CPCU designation. Copies of the CPCU key are available from the American Institute for reproduction in such advertisements. These advertisements must be strictly congratulatory in nature, however, and should not include the business conducted by the firm, the lines of insurance carried by the firm, the firm's telephone number, or any copy soliciting business.

c. The designation Chartered Property Casualty Underwriter, the initials CPCU, and the CPCU key may be used by the CPCU Society in a manner that complies with the Rules and Guidelines of the American Institute's Code of Professional Ethics and that has first been authorized in writing by the Ethics Counsel of the American Institute.

d. The designation Chartered Property Casualty Underwriter, the initials CPCU, and the CPCU key may not be used in any manner that violates a Rule of the Code of Professional Ethics. Rules R8.2, R8.3, and R8.4 deserve special mention in this context since they relate directly to, and impose restrictions upon, the privilege to use the CPCU designation.

e. The designation Chartered Property Casualty Underwriter, the initials CPCU, and the CPCU key may be used in any other manner that has received prior approval in writing from the Ethics Counsel of the American Institute.

G8.2 Rule R8.2 stipulates that "A CPCU shall not attribute to the mere possession of the designation depth or scope of knowledge, skills, and professional capabilities greater than those demonstrated by successful completion of the CPCU program." Unless this Rule is strictly observed by all CPCUs, the public will be misled and the integrity of the designation, as well as the integrity of the violator, will be significantly diminished. The public is protected and the integrity of the designation and its holder are best preserved by avoiding any misrepresentations of the nature and significance of the CPCU designation.

CANON 9

CPCUs should assist in maintaining the integrity of the Code of Professional Ethics.

Rules of Professional Conduct

R9.1   A CPCU shall not initiate or support the CPCU candidacy of any individual he or she knows engages in business practices that violate the ethical standards prescribed by this Code.

R9.2   A CPCU possessing unprivileged information concerning an alleged violation of this Code shall, upon request, reveal such information to the tribunal or other authority empowered by the American Institute to investigate or act upon the alleged violation.

R9.3   A CPCU shall report promptly to the American Institute any information concerning the use of the CPCU designation by an unauthorized person.

Guidelines for Professional Conduct

G9.1   A CPCU should assist in upholding the experience, educational, and ethical standards prescribed for prospective CPCU designees by the American Institute.

G9.2   A CPCU should assist the American Institute in preserving the integrity of the Code, first and foremost, by voluntarily complying with both the letter and the spirit of the Code. Ultimately, however, the public can be protected and the integrity of the Code can be maintained only if the Code is strictly but fairly enforced, and this, in turn, can be achieved only if Code violations are promptly brought to the attention of the proper officials. Although a CPCU should not become a self-appointed investigator or judge on matters properly left to the BEI, every CPCU should comply with the mandates of Rules R9.1, R9.2, and R9.3. Except for the comparatively rare but troublesome situation covered by R9.3, whether a CPCU should volunteer adverse information is left to the CPCU's judgment.

G9.3   Upon request, a CPCU should serve on committees, boards, or tribunals prescribed by the American Institute for the administration or enforcement of the Code. A CPCU is obligated to disqualify himself or herself from such service if the CPCU believes, in good conscience, that he or she could not serve in a fair and an impartial manner or upon request.

Commentary on the Canons, Rules, and Guidelines of the Code of Professional Ethics

CHAPTER

3

This chapter examines the Canons, Rules, and Guidelines of the Code of Professional Ethics of the American Institute for CPCU (the Code), along with relevant published Advisory Opinions. The official wording of the Code and formal position statements appear in boldfaced type. The accompanying discussion and examples are informal commentary.

CANON 1 – ALTRUISM

CPCUs should endeavor at all times to place the public interest above their own.

The essence of this Canon is altruism. Altruism is unselfish concern for the welfare of others (selflessness.) In ethics, it is the doctrine that the general welfare of society is the proper goal of an individual's actions: opposed to egoism.[1]

The Code's fundamental objective is to serve the public interest. Other Canons, along with the Rules and Guidelines, clarify "the public interest" and how CPCUs should endeavor to put it first.

Rule R1.1 – Duty to Understand and Abide by All Rules

A CPCU has a duty to understand and abide by all Rules of conduct prescribed in the Code of Professional Ethics (the Code).

The Canons establish goals. The Rules specify minimum standards of behavior. Violation of Rule R1.1 or any other Rule can lead to sanctions against a CPCU or candidate.

This Rule may appear unnecessary because failure to abide by any other Rule constitutes grounds for a sanction under the Code. Moreover, a CPCU would be unlikely to be formally charged with a Code violation solely because he or she does not understand the Rules. Rule R1.1 does, however, serve two roles. First, it introduces the other Rules by specifying that CPCUs are obligated to understand and abide by them. Second, it prevents a CPCU charged with violation of another Rule from using ignorance of the Rules as a defense. Any CPCU who claims he or she cannot be charged with a Rules violation because he or she did not understand the Rules has violated Rule R1.1.

Rule R1.2 – Actions by Others

A CPCU shall not advocate, sanction, participate in, cause to be accomplished, otherwise carry out through another, or condone any act the CPCU is prohibited from performing by the Rules of the Code.

The Rules apply to both a CPCU's actions and to others' actions. CPCUs who act through others to accomplish what they cannot ethically do on their own are as guilty as if they had committed the unethical act themselves. Rule R1.2 further specifies that CPCUs also should not sanction or condone actions that would be unethical if committed by a CPCU. At minimum, a CPCU should protest unethical activities.

Guidelines

Guidelines help to interpret the Rules and clarify the Canons' goals. The Guidelines are not binding. Generally, CPCUs and candidates cannot be sanctioned for failure to meet the Guidelines' standards.

Guideline G1.1 – The Public Interest

By stipulating that CPCUs should endeavor at all times to place the public interest above their own, Canon 1 serves as the fundamental goal of the entire Code. The other Code standards define the "public interest" (and hence the ethical obligations of CPCUs) more specifically.

CPCUs can place the public interest above their own by understanding and obeying all the Rules in the Code (as specified in R1.1 and R1.2) and then, beyond the expected minimums, by striving to meet the standards expressed in the Canons and the Guidelines. A formal commitment to altruism is probably the single most important characteristic that defines professional behavior.

This Guideline reiterates the importance of placing the public interest above one's own. All CPCUs should strive to abide by this Canon.

Guideline G1.2 – Conflicts of Interest

A CPCU should avoid even the appearance of impropriety when performing his or her professional duties and should act in a manner that ultimately will best serve his or her own professional interests. This Guideline, followed in conjunction with the other provisions of the Code, should pose no insurmountable problems of priority in most situations because a CPCU's best long-term professional interests ordinarily do not conflict either with the public interest or with other specific interests. However, potential conflicts of interest may arise, or may appear to arise, because many CPCUs simultaneously must balance multiple professional interests with their personal interests and the best interests of the general public. For example, a CPCU employed by an insurer may serve his or her immediate superior, the corporation, the stockholders, the policyholders, agents, and industry associations. An agent may serve his or her clients; two or more insurers; and his or her business partners, stockholders, or associates.

Strict compliance with all the Rules of the Code, including R1.2, should enable a CPCU to resolve such potential conflicts of interest. However, when a person subject to the Code is uncertain about the ethical propriety of a specific activity or type of conduct, he or she should refrain from engaging in the questionable activity or conduct until the matter has been clarified. Any CPCU or CPCU candidate who needs assistance in interpreting the Code is encouraged to request an advisory opinion from the American Institute's Board of Ethical Inquiry (BEI).

The standards of professional conduct require more than avoiding improper behavior. G1.2 calls for avoiding even the appearance of impropriety. It also acknowledges that the professional roles of many CPCUs appear to present inherent conflicts of interest.

Other professionals also face conflicts of interest. For example, physicians must provide appropriate healthcare services to their patients while serving the administrative requirements of managed care organizations. Likewise, accountants hired to examine an organization's financial records according to generally accepted accounting principles may uncover issues that reflect poorly on the organization that hires them but that must nonetheless be included in their report.

To avoid ethical impropriety in the face of conflicting priorities, G1.2 suggests first that a CPCU act in a manner that best serves his or her long-term professional interests and avoid even the appearance of impropriety. G1.2 also advises that CPCUs refrain from potentially unethical activities until they receive clarification of the activity's permissibility. One may also request the BEI to provide assistance in interpreting the Code. Such requests should be directed to the Ethics Counsel at the American Institute. The resulting clarification usually is presented as an informal advisory opinion.

Guideline G1.3 – Applicable to All CPCUs (and Candidates)

The ethical obligation to place the public interest above personal interests or financial gain extends to every CPCU, regardless of whether the CPCU's occupational position requires direct contact with actual or prospective insurance consumers.

Producers, claim representatives, and others with direct customer contact have the most obvious opportunities for conflicts of interest. This Guideline emphasizes that CPCUs in almost every function can face situations in which they are tempted to place their own interests, or others' interests, above the public interest.

Guideline G1.4 – Preferential Treatment

The Guidelines do not imply that insurance purchasers should be given preferential treatment over insurance claimants because the needs and best interests of insurance purchasers are in fact served only when all insurance claimants, including third-party liability claimants, are accorded prompt, equitable, and otherwise fair treatment.

Placing the public interest above one's own may suggest that CPCUs ought to provide benefits to which some people are not entitled. This Guideline clarifies that the public interest is best served when all parties receive fair treatment.

Other Related Code Provisions

Many of the Code's provisions are closely linked. This is especially so with Canon 1 because altruism is the foundation of the entire Code. Also, because they mention other Rules, R1.1 and R1.2 are linked to every other Rule.

Relevant Hypothetical Case Studies

Hypothetical Case Studies (HCSs) illustrate ways in which the Code's drafters envisioned its application. The HCSs also demonstrate the interrelationships among various Code provisions. The following HCSs address Canon 1 and its related provisions:

- HCS 102
- HCS 103
- HCS 105
- HCS 114
- HCS 119

Questions to Consider

1. What is altruism?
2. Why is altruism the one characteristic that most distinguishes professional behavior from unprofessional behavior?
3. How should CPCUs place the public interest above their own?

Suggested Answers

1. Altruism is unselfish concern for the welfare of others.
2. Altruism is the one characteristic that most distinguishes professional behavior from unprofessional behavior because professionalism involves serving the public interest.
3. CPCUs should place others' interests above their own by doing their utmost to live up to the high aspirational standards expressed in the Canons.

CANON 2 – CONTINUING PROFESSIONAL DEVELOPMENT

CPCUs should seek continually to maintain and improve their professional knowledge, skills, and competence.

This is the only Canon that has just one Rule. While the Canon sets a high goal that includes improving professional knowledge, skills, and competence, Rule R2.1 clarifies that each CPCU must, at a minimum, maintain competence in his or her area of responsibility.

Rule R2.1 – Maintaining Professional Competence

A CPCU shall keep informed on technical matters that are essential to the maintenance of the CPCU's professional competence in insurance, risk management, or related fields.

Canon 2 emphasizes that professionals should never stop learning. CPCUs should continually try to serve the public interest by improving their abilities through a combination of education and experience. CPCUs are required to keep informed on the matters that are essential to their competent performance as insurance or risk management professionals—or, if applicable, in the related field in which they practice.

The implications of CPCU competence extend beyond service to customers, colleagues, and professional contacts. Other issues relating to maintaining the integrity of the CPCU designation are discussed in connection with Canon 8.

Guidelines

The Guidelines elaborate on these points.

Guideline G2.1 – Ethical Obligation for Continuous Learning

Though knowledge and skills alone do not ensure that an individual will adhere to high ethical standards, they are requisites to the high levels of competence and performance expected of all professionals. This is especially true for practitioners in a business such as insurance, which is characterized not only by its existing complexities but also by rapid changes in the business and in the legal, economic, and social environments in which it operates. If an individual purports to be a professional and yet does not maintain high levels of competence and performance, he or she engages in unethical conduct. Therefore, every CPCU has an ethical obligation to engage actively and continuously in appropriate educational activities.

This Guideline clarifies that continuously improving performance is more than just good practice. CPCUs have an ethical obligation to continuously learn.

Guideline G2.2 – A Matter of Individual Judgment

At a minimum, as specified in Rule R2.1, "A CPCU shall keep informed on technical matters that are essential to the maintenance of his or her professional competence in insurance, risk management, or related fields." Because CPCUs serve as agents, brokers, underwriters, claim representatives, actuaries, risk managers, regulators, company executives, and specialists in a wide variety of insurance-related fields, the Rule does not attempt to prescribe the specific technical matters that are essential to the maintenance of professional competence in each of the numerous specialties. Instead, a CPCU must decide, in the light of his or her occupational position, the content and form of continuing education that will satisfy R2.1.

A single set of standards cannot be applied to the vast array of occupations in which CPCUs are engaged. Each CPCU may use professional judgment to determine how best to meet his or her ethical obligations that satisfy R2.1 and aspire to the goals of Canon 2.

Guideline G2.3 – No Mandatory Recertification

Many professions have established mandatory continuing education requirements that impose severe penalties on members who do not periodically certify that they have met at least one of the specified continuing education options. The trustees of the American Institute have no plans to require CPCUs to certify periodically that they have met the obligations under Rule R2.1. However, the maintenance of professional competence is considered a minimum obligation of every CPCU. The BEI will investigate alleged violations of Rule R2.1 and may impose warranted penalties on violators. Furthermore, if a CPCU is accused of violating any other Rule, the Board may, at its discretion, require the accused to furnish evidence of compliance with Rule R2.1.

Rule R2.1 clarifies that CPCUs have an ethical obligation to continuously learn. Any CPCU who fails to comply with a Rule can be sanctioned by the BEI. Because R2.1 requires CPCUs to keep informed, it implies that CPCUs could be sanctioned for failure to meet a continuing education standard. Such a sanction, however, is unlikely. If a CPCU's inadequate performance leads to an ethics complaint, R2.1 may be one of several rules considered by the BEI in determining appropriate action.

Guideline G2.4 – Continuing Professional Development (CPD) Program

Beyond the minimum continuing education requirements referred to in Rule R2.1, all CPCUs are urged to engage in additional pursuits that will meet the aspirational goal, under Canon 2, of improving their professional knowledge, skills, and competence.

For example, the BEI suggests that every CPCU qualify for recognition under the Continuing Professional Development (CPD) program, which is jointly sponsored by the American Institute and the CPCU Society.

The CPD program recognizes those who have met specific criteria. The requirements of the CPD program, which are occasionally revised, are automatically distributed to members of the CPCU Society and are available to others on request. Points are assigned to various activities. Current criteria include the following:

- Passing an exam or a course in a respected insurance or business-related program
- Passing a college or university course in insurance, risk management, or a business-related subject
- Teaching a course in insurance, risk management, or a business-related subject
- Authoring or coauthoring an article accepted for publication in the *CPCU e-Journal* or similar business publication, a CPCU Society section newsletter, or a textbook
- Conducting a research project
- Serving as an officer, a director, a committee chair, or a committee member of a national insurance organization or local CPCU chapter
- Serving as a class coordinator for a CPCU chapter or another course-sponsoring organization
- Serving on a state insurance advisory committee
- Grading CPCU or Insurance Institute of America (IIA) exams
- Serving on exam-development committees for CPCU, IIA, state licensing, or other examination programs
- Attending the CPCU Annual Meeting and Seminars or the annual meetings of other national insurance organizations
- Attending educational meetings, seminars, videoconferences, or workshops sponsored by the CPCU Society or others
- Attending meetings of CPCU chapters or other insurance organizations that include a speaker or an educational program
- Meeting state continuing education requirements for licensing
- Being an expert witness
- Serving as a personal sponsor for CPCU and IIA students

The CPD program is a voluntary recognition program. It enables CPCUs who record their participation to receive recognition for their activities.

Professionals use a myriad of formal and informal learning experiences to improve their professional skills, knowledge, and competence. Canon 2's intent is not to deemphasize the importance of formal education, but to acknowledge all types of relevant learning.

A CPCU who has little opportunity to learn on the job and who makes no effort to learn outside of the work environment does not reflect favorably on his or her profession or on the CPCU designation. The Institute would not initiate action against a CPCU in such circumstances but would respond to any charges brought under the Code in an appropriate complaint.

All CPCUs are obligated to maintain the skills necessary to perform their job competently. A CPCU who is not active in the insurance and risk management workforce would not be required to forfeit the CPCU designation. However, any CPCU should adhere to Rule R8.2, which requires a CPCU to avoid overstating his or her current level of expertise.

A retired CPCU who, for example, acts as an expert witness in insurance cases, operates as an insurance and risk management consultant, or teaches insurance classes, would be expected to remain informed and competent on matters with which he or she is involved. A nonretired CPCU who exits the workforce would not have an ethical obligation to maintain current insurance skills as long as he or she is not active in the insurance business. However, any CPCU returning to the insurance/risk management workforce after a long absence would have an ethical obligation to avoid situations that require more current knowledge than he or she possesses, as well as an obligation to become informed to meet current responsibilities.

Professional standards are not limited to those who have agreed to be bound by the Code. However, those who are not bound by the Code are not subject to sanctions under the Code.

Although the Code and the CPD both deal with the professional development of CPCUs, there is no direct relationship between them.

- The Code states the ethical responsibilities of all CPCUs. It also describes a system for censuring those who do not live up to their responsibilities.
- The CPD program is a reward program that recognizes CPCUs who have met certain criteria established by the program. The criteria of the CPD program are partially based on Guideline G2.4 of the Code.

Other Related Code Provisions

Canon 2, along with its associated Rules and Guidelines, is closely related to other Code provisions, as follows:

- According to Canon 2, CPCUs should "seek continually to maintain and improve their…competence." Competence is again specified in Rule R4.1: "A CPCU shall competently…discharge his or her occupational duties." G4.1 notes that CPCUs maintain their professional competence by keeping informed. Keeping informed results in the competence that is necessary to "consistently discharge…occupational duties."

- According to Canon 2, CPCUs should seek continually to maintain and improve their professional knowledge and skills. G6.4 states that knowledge and skills are necessary for CPCUs to exercise independent judgment and to recognize their limitations.

- A professional's current knowledge involves more than the skills required for job performance. G7.2 directs CPCUs to keep abreast of legislation, changing conditions, and/or other developments that affect the insuring public and assist in keeping the public informed of them.

- G7.3 notes that CPCUs can contribute to a better public understanding of insurance and risk management only if they maintain and improve their own knowledge and communication skills.

- After completing the courses necessary to earn the CPCU designation, CPCUs are ethically obligated to continuously learn. However, R8.2 and G8.2 forbid CPCUs from conveying the impression that holding the CPCU designation, by itself, implies a level of knowledge, skills, or capabilities beyond those required to complete the CPCU program. In short, professional knowledge, skills, and competence provide the tools without which a professional cannot fulfill other responsibilities.

Relevant Hypothetical Case Studies

The following HCSs deal in some manner with Canon 2 and related provisions:

- HCS 102
- HCS 104
- HCS 110
- HCS 112
- HCS 113
- HCS 117

Questions to Consider

1. Why is it unethical for a person who does not maintain high levels of professional competence to claim to be a professional?

2. Why is it especially important that a CPCU maintain the competence developed through CPCU studies and other professional studies?

3. What is the minimum standard a CPCU should meet in maintaining professional competence?

4. What types of activities will help CPCUs meet the aspirational goal of improving professional knowledge, skills, and competence?

Suggested Answers

1. It is unethical for a person who does not maintain high levels of professional competence to claim to be a professional because any person claiming abilities he or she does not possess misrepresents himself or herself to the people with whom he or she deals.

2. Maintaining the competence developed through CPCU studies is essential to remain a professional.

3. The minimum standard a CPCU should meet is to remain informed on technical matters that are essential to maintain competence in his or her particular position in insurance or risk management.

4. Taking or teaching CPCU and IIA courses or other insurance/risk management courses, teaching similar courses, writing articles, conducting research, or performing other similar activities will help CPCUs meet the aspirational goal of improving professional knowledge, skills, and competence.

CANON 3 – LEGAL CONDUCT

CPCUs should obey all laws and regulations, and should avoid any conduct or activity that would cause unjust harm to others.

The first part of Canon 3 is not an especially lofty goal. Everybody is expected to obey laws and regulations. Failure to do so can lead to legal and administrative sanctions. The second part addresses the distinction between harm and unjust harm. Some legal, ethical, and just conduct results in harm to others. For example, if a family's claim clearly is not covered by insurance, a claim representative ought to deny payment even if the family is impoverished by the loss. To do otherwise would be unjust (see Guideline G1.4). However, it is often difficult to recognize—particularly in advance—the ways in which an activity may affect others.

To date, every case in which a CPCU's designation has been suspended or revoked has involved a violation of one or more Rules under Canon 3, often in conjunction with other Rules violations.

Rule R3.1 – Dishonesty, Deceit, Fraud

In the conduct of business or professional activities, a CPCU shall not engage in any act or omission of a dishonest, deceitful, or fraudulent nature.

Dishonesty, deceit, or fraud violate this rule, regardless of whether they involve the violation of a law or regulation. Each of the following cases in which the BEI revoked an individual's CPCU designation involved an alleged violation of Rule 3.1. In most cases, other rules were also violated.

- A producer allegedly obtained money by telling an insurance purchaser that the purchaser would be covered by an insurance policy issued by an insurance company that, in fact, did not exist.

- A producer misappropriated premium monies from a consumer. As a result of these charges, his licenses were revoked and he was sentenced to prison. Upon his release from prison, he circulated a resume indicating that he held the CPCU designation, despite it having been revoked. The BEI threatened legal action if he did not cease and desist.

- A producer collected a substantial premium payment from the insured but failed to remit it to the insurer. As a consequence, his license was revoked by the state insurance commissioner.

- A producer misappropriated premium refunds due to policyholders. He consented to revocation of his license and a fine.

- A claim manager awarded repair work in connection with a large number of claims to various building contractors in exchange for a 15-percent kickback. He was convicted on thirteen counts of mail fraud, conspiracy, extortion, and income tax evasion; sentenced to a prison term; and fined.

- A claim adjuster admitted that he had violated the Code by misappropriating his employer's funds through a variety of ruses, including making false claims payments and pocketing the proceeds of sold salvaged property.

- A CPCU who served as president of a savings and loan association pled guilty in court to embezzling over a million dollars from the association.

Guideline G3.1 – Misrepresentation or Concealment

A CPCU should neither misrepresent nor conceal a fact or information that is material to determining the suitability, efficacy, scope, or limitations of an insurance contract or a surety bond. Nor should a CPCU materially misrepresent or conceal the financial condition, or the quality of services, of any insurer or reinsurer. The extent to which a CPCU should volunteer information and facts must necessarily be left to sound professional judgment. This Guideline illustrates the kinds of acts and omissions that can be "dishonest, deceitful, or fraudulent," in violation of Rule R3.1, and that normally "would cause unjust harm to others," thus violating the spirit of Canon 3.

Although G3.1 relates most clearly to dishonesty, deceit, or fraud, it may also apply in situations in which the pursuit of financial gain or other personal benefit may undermine sound professional judgment—in violation of Rule R3.2.

Rule R3.2 – Financial Gain, Personal Benefit

A CPCU shall not allow the pursuit of financial gain or other personal benefit to interfere with the exercise of sound professional judgment and skills.

Many of the most serious charges against CPCUs, including those cited under Rule R3.1, include an alleged violation of Rule R3.2, typically accompanied by other alleged Rule violations. Such charges usually involve the use of money to which the CPCU is not entitled. For example, one CPCU's designation was revoked for retaining premium refunds to policyholders for his own benefit. However, R3.2 encompasses not only monetary gain but also other personal benefit.

Rule R3.3 – Violation of Law or Regulation; Conviction of a Felony

A CPCU shall not violate any law or regulation relating to professional activities or commit any felony.

R3.3 is the only Rule whose violation may lead to an immediate suspension of the CPCU designation. This information is not included in the body of the Code but in the Disciplinary Rules, Procedures, and Penalties, as follows:

> A CPCU convicted by verdict, guilty plea, or plea of nolo contendere, of any crime that violates the Rules of Professional Conduct immediately loses the right to use the CPCU designation. Such suspension of the right to use the CPCU designation shall last indefinitely, or until the convicted party petitions the Board of Ethical Inquiry and convinces the Board of that party's fitness again to use the designation.

Automatic suspension applies to conviction of any crime that violates the Rules of Professional Conduct. The following two crimes fall into this category:

1. Violation of a law relating to professional activities
2. Commission of a felony

Notice the position of the phrase "relating to professional activities." CPCUs violate the Code if they commit any felony, regardless of whether it relates to their professional activities. A CPCU who otherwise violates a law or regulation not relating to professional activities is not necessarily in violation of the Code. For example, unless other Rules are involved, a speeding ticket or a charge of public drunkenness would not provide grounds for action under the Code.

CPCUs are subject to regulations promulgated by state insurance departments and other regulatory bodies. Automatic suspension applies to conviction of a crime, not violation of a regulation. A CPCU who violates a regulation relating to professional activities is in violation of Rule R3.3, but his or her designation will not automatically be suspended without further investigation. Guideline G3.3 notes that ignorance is not a defense. CPCUs should be aware of all regulations to which they are subject, and they are obligated to adhere to them. However, the BEI will not sanction a CPCU for violation of a regulation without further investigation and evaluation of the circumstances.

The distinctions among laws, regulations, crimes of different degrees, and professional and nonprofessional activities are summarized as follows:

- Violation of an insurance law or regulation relates to professional activities but is not a crime. A candidate or CPCU who violates such laws or regulations may be disciplined, but he or she is not subject to automatic suspension.
- Conviction of any crime relating to professional activities, including misdemeanors, automatically subjects a candidate or CPCU to immediate suspension.

- Conviction of a felony, regardless of whether it is related to professional activities, automatically subjects a candidate to immediate suspension.

Guideline G3.2 – Unfair Competition

A CPCU should not, to the detriment of the insuring public, engage in any business practice or activity designed to restrict fair competition. However, this Guideline does not prohibit a CPCU's participation in a legally enforceable covenant not to compete, or in a similar activity specifically sanctioned or required by law.

While unfair competition may be illegal, unethical, or both, fair competition is the basis of the free enterprise system. People often disagree about what constitutes fair competition. Insurance is a competitive business, and activities that restrict competition can cause unjust harm to the public. However, some collaborative activities are necessary, legally sanctioned, or required, and therefore appropriate. Two such examples are as follows:

EXAMPLE

Agreement Not to Compete

A covenant not to compete is a contractual agreement under which one party agrees not to compete with another party. For example, the party selling an insurance agency to a buyer may agree not to engage in insurance sales in the same geographic area as the agency for a stated time period. Similar contractual agreements are common among independent agents. A new insurance producer, for example, may be required to sign a covenant agreeing not to sell insurance to the same clients, for another agency, within fifty miles for a two-year period after terminating her relationship with her current employer. Although such a covenant restricts a party's rights, it is part of the consideration involved in the contract. A covenant not to compete is generally legal and enforceable, and entering into such a covenant or enforcing one does not constitute a violation of the Code. Breach of contract, in violation of a covenant not to compete, may involve violation of one or more Rules of the Code. Disputes over these covenants or other civil disputes frequently involve significant questions of fact and are best resolved by pursuing other remedies.

EXAMPLE

Insurance Advisory Organizations

Insurance advisory organizations maintain centralized pools of loss data that are used by insurers to set their rates and to develop standard policy contract forms. All insurance companies that use these services may offer a similar product and similar pricing. Some argue that this type of collaboration inhibits fair competition; others believe competition would be limited if insurers did not have the pool of data or standard policy forms on which sound pricing decisions can be based. In any case, insurance advisory organizations are sanctioned or required by law, and mere participation in an insurance advisory organization is not a violation of the Code.

Guideline G3.3 – Inappropriate Compensation

When performing his or her occupational function, a CPCU should not, at the expense of the uninformed, deliberately achieve or seek to achieve financial gain for the CPCU or the CPCU's employer that is unconscionable relative to the customary gains for the quantity and quality of services actually rendered.

Generally, no CPCU should seek or accept compensation that is neither for nor commensurate with professional services actually rendered or to be rendered. Nor should any CPCU seek or accept compensation under any other terms, conditions, or circumstances that would violate any Canon, Rule, or Guideline in this Code. However, nothing in this Guideline prohibits seeking or accepting gifts from family or personal friends, income from investments, or income from any other activity that would neither prevent nor inherently impair the free and complete exercise of the CPCU's sound professional judgment and skills nor otherwise violate the Code.

A CPCU should not perform professional services under terms, conditions, or circumstances that would prevent or inherently impair the free and complete exercise of the CPCU's sound professional judgment and skills. This Guideline does not prohibit a CPCU from being compensated under the terms of a legally acceptable commission arrangement, because such an arrangement does not prevent or inherently impair the CPCU's professional judgment and skills. But it does serve to remind a CPCU so compensated of his or her ethical obligation to avoid any recommendation to a consumer of the CPCU's services that would increase the CPCU's compensation, unless such recommendation clearly meets the consumer's legitimate needs and best interests. The Guideline also serves to remind every CPCU, regardless of his or her basis of compensation, of the ethical obligation to render fully such services as are contemplated and rightfully owed under the terms of the applicable compensation arrangement.

CPCUs should not overcharge for their services. Vastly different opinions may exist as to the worth of a person's services, but this Guideline clarifies that unconscionable charges well outside the customary charges for similar services are inappropriate, especially if they seek to exploit an uninformed consumer.

It is inappropriate to solicit or accept bribes in exchange for a favor, whether that favor involves paying a claim, accepting an application, or performing other services. G3.3 emphasizes that inappropriate compensation or gifts should not affect a CPCU's judgment or skills. In fact, a CPCU should not perform professional services under circumstances in which his or her professional judgment is constrained.

G3.3 also emphasizes that while commission income (reimbursement as a percentage of sales) is appropriate, CPCUs ought to avoid recommendations that would increase their income but would not also clearly serve the customer's best interests.

Guideline G3.4 – Awareness of Applicable Laws and Regulations

While the American Institute's standards of ethical conduct are not limited to the duties and obligations imposed upon CPCUs by the laws and regulations governing the conduct of all insurance practitioners, obedience to and respect for law and regulatory authority are absolute minimum standards of professional conduct. The potential consequences of violating this admonition extend beyond those that may fall upon the violator, because one CPCU's violation of laws or regulations may discredit the CPCU designation itself.

A CPCU is obligated to keep informed of every law and regulation governing or otherwise pertaining to his or her business activities and, when necessary, should seek interpretive assistance from the appropriate regulatory officials and/or retain the services of competent legal counsel. If a CPCU doubts the legality of a particular kind of business conduct or activity, he or she should refrain from such conduct or activity. A CPCU may not plead lack of knowledge as a defense for improper conduct under Rule R3.3 unless he or she can demonstrate that a reasonable, good-faith effort was made to obtain such knowledge, and it was not available.

Because legal requirements provide a minimum behavioral standard, violation of R3.3 may lead to automatic suspension. As G3.4 suggests, a CPCU who violates laws or regulations undermines all CPCUs. When a CPCU is charged with or convicted of some violation, an officer of the local CPCU chapter may contact the American Institute's Ethics Counsel and initiate a complaint so that the offender can be disciplined, if such an action is applicable. The local CPCU chapter may also contact the CPCU Society to initiate a complaint so that the offender is removed from the rolls of the CPCU chapter.

Other Related Code Provisions

Canon 3, along with its associated Rules and Guidelines, is closely related to other Code provisions, as follows:

- Obeying laws and regulations and avoiding unjust activity clearly relate to the precepts of Canon 1 that involve placing the public interest above one's own.

- R1.2 clarifies that any CPCU who does not personally violate R3.1, R3.2, or R3.3 but condones others' violations is in violation of the Code.

- To avoid breaking a law or violating a regulation, CPCUs must keep informed, as indicated in Canon 2 and R2.1.

- The best way for a CPCU to avoid any conduct or activity that would cause unjust harm to others is to have the knowledge, skills, and competence necessary to recognize the implications of his or her actions. This requires keeping informed through continuous learning, in keeping with Canon 2 and R2.1.

Relevant Hypothetical Case Studies

The following HCSs deal in some manner with Canon 3 and related provisions:

- HCS 101
- HCS 102
- HCS 103
- HCS 104
- HCS 105
- HCS 106
- HCS 107
- HCS 109
- HCS 110
- HCS 111
- HCS 113
- HCS 114
- HCS 115
- HCS 116
- HCS 117
- HCS 118
- HCS 119
- HCS 122

Questions to Consider

1. Naturally, CPCUs are expected to refrain from illegal activities, but legality is generally considered a minimum standard of behavior. How do the aspirational goals of Canon 3 go beyond encouraging legal behavior?
2. Are CPCUs subject to discipline for illegal conduct outside the scope of their business conduct? Explain.
3. Under what circumstances is a CPCU to be held responsible for violating a law or regulation about which he or she was unaware?

Suggested Answers

1. Canon 3 requires CPCUs, in addition to obeying laws and regulations, not to cause unjust harm to others.
2. CPCUs are subject to discipline for illegal conduct outside the scope of their business conduct. Any CPCU convicted of a felony is subject to automatic suspension of his or her CPCU designation.
3. Because CPCUs are responsible for knowing the laws and regulations to which they are subject, they always are held responsible for violating a law or regulation about which they were unaware.

▶▶

CANON 4 – DILIGENT PERFORMANCE

CPCUs should be diligent in the performance of their occupational duties and should continually strive to improve the functioning of the insurance mechanism.

This Canon consists of two parts. The first entails behavior on the job, and the second involves a CPCU's effect on the risk management and insurance environment. These two parts are reflected in the two Rules that fall under Canon 4. R4.1 addresses occupational duties, while R4.2 deals with improving the insurance mechanism.

These two parts are sometimes related. The work of some CPCUs directly affects the insurance environment. Examples include those involved in product development, research, or regulation. The day-to-day activities of other CPCUs have little direct effect on the insurance mechanism as a whole but should still be performed with diligence.

Rule R4.1 – Performing Occupational Duties

A CPCU shall competently and consistently discharge his or her occupational duties.

Guideline G4.1 – Employment, Contractual, and Civil Disputes Involving Diligent Performance

The public expects both competence and diligence from professionals. Thus, to complement Rule R2.1, which obligates a CPCU to maintain professional competence by keeping informed, Rule R4.1 stipulates that "a CPCU shall competently and consistently discharge his or her occupational duties."

Although the BEI believes that all professionals, including CPCUs, should perform diligently, it will not intervene or arbitrate between the parties in an employment, or a contractual, relationship or a civil dispute. Nor are the American Institute's disciplinary procedures a substitute for legal and other remedies available to such parties. In the event of an alleged violation of Rule R4.1, therefore, the Board will hear the case only after all other remedies have been exhausted, and it generally will take disciplinary action only in circumstances in which a proven violation has caused unjust harm to another person, and the violation brings substantial discredit upon the CPCU designation; or it would otherwise be in the public interest to take disciplinary action under the Code.

Notice the direct relationship between Rule R2.1 and Rule R4.1. A professional cannot competently discharge his or her duties without also keeping informed of all factors that affect those duties. As previously noted, a CPCU probably would not be sanctioned under the Code merely for failure to keep current. However, such failure is inevitably reflected in job performance and could therefore lead to violation of both R4.1 and R2.1.

The authors of the Code recognized that the disciplinary actions for violating the ethical obligation of diligent performance had to be qualified in the Guidelines to prevent the American Institute from becoming an intervener or arbitrator in contractual or civil disputes with employers, principals, or clients. G4.1 clarifies that the Code is neither a remedy for employer-employee disputes nor a remedy for other disputes better settled through legal procedures and other remedies. The BEI will not become involved in such disputes until other remedies have been exhausted.

Determining what constitutes "diligent performance" can be highly subjective, especially when promotions, performance evaluations, salary adjustments, and other elements of the work environment are involved. Interpersonal disputes, regardless of whether they involve employment, contracts, or civil law, often generate conflict. A person who feels wronged might seek retribution against the alleged wrongdoer by filing an ethics complaint.

A disciplinary action does not fix such problems. If a contract has been breached, for example, the more effective remedy is to seek to enforce the contract, not to seek a reprimand or other action from the BEI.

Because it is presented in connection with Canon 4, G4.1 applies most specifically to the performance of occupational duties. However, the principle discussed in G4.1 applies to other types of activities as well. The enforcement provisions of the Code are not an appropriate substitute for legal or other remedies available in many cases.

Rule R4.2 – Improving the Insurance Mechanism

A CPCU shall support efforts to effect improvements in claim settlement, contract design, investment, marketing, pricing, reinsurance, safety engineering, underwriting, and other insurance operations that will both benefit the public and improve the overall efficiency with which the insurance mechanism functions.

The Guidelines demonstrate how CPCUs can support efforts to improve the insurance mechanism through examples that focus on policy language, financial integrity, availability, efficiency, humanitarianism, and support for research. However, CPCU efforts to improve risk management and insurance are not limited to these areas.

Guideline G4.2 – Improving the Insurance Mechanism

Because Guidelines G4.3 through G4.8 clarify the principles in G4.2, they are also discussed in the context of Guideline G4.2, as follows:

In addition to competently and consistently discharging his or her own occupational duties, a CPCU is obligated by Rule R4.2 "to support efforts to effect such improvements [in insurer functions and operations] that will both benefit the public and improve the overall efficiency with which the insurance mechanism functions." This emphasizes that it is possible to

effect improvements in insurer efficiency and profitability in a manner contrary to the public interest. It is sometimes difficult to determine whether a proposed change will both improve overall efficiency and benefit the public, but the CPCU's ethical obligation, consistent with the theme expressed in Canon 1, is to support efforts to effect such improvements. The kinds of efforts that satisfy both criteria, and that the Board believes a CPCU should support, are illustrated in the following Guidelines:

Guideline G4.3 – Policy Language

A CPCU should assist in improving the language, suitability, adaptability, and general efficacy of insurance contracts and surety bonds.

Guideline G4.4 – Financial Integrity

A CPCU should assist in ensuring protection and security for the public, and in maintaining and improving the integrity of the insurance institution, by helping to preserve and improve the financial strength of all private insurers.

Guideline G4.5 – Availability

A CPCU should assist in providing an adequate supply of insurance and surety bonds to meet public demands and needs.

Guideline G4.6 – Efficiency

A CPCU should assist in minimizing the cost to the public of insurance and suretyship, without compromising the quality of benefits or services provided, by helping to improve the operational efficiency of insurers and their representatives by contributing to the solution of economic, legal, political, and other social problems that demonstrably increase the cost of insurance and suretyship without enhancing quality or otherwise improving public well-being. Examples of such problems include inflation, unemployment, crime, inequities and inefficiencies in the legal system, inequities and inefficiencies in the healthcare delivery system, floods, and other natural catastrophes. The availability of insurance alone will not solve such problems. However, a CPCU should not neglect his or her personal duty to become actively involved in the search for underlying causes of, and long-term solutions to, such problems.

Guideline G4.7 – Humanitarianism and Loss Control

Because of a CPCU's professional capabilities and knowledge of the magnitude of human and dollar losses suffered annually, he or she should assume an especially active role in private and public loss-prevention and loss-reduction efforts. A CPCU should do the utmost to preserve human life; maintain and improve the physical and mental health of all human beings; and prevent the damage, destruction, and abstraction of property.

Guideline G4.8 – Support for Research

A CPCU should participate in and support research that helps to improve the private insurance mechanism and research that helps to reduce losses of life, health, or property.

CPCUs often can do the following to help improve the insurance mechanism:

- Improve insurance and surety contracts
- Maintain the financial strength and integrity of risk financing systems
- Help ensure the availability of insurance, surety bonds, and alternative risk financing systems
- Improve efficiency and otherwise help minimize the cost of insurance and other so-called costs of risk
- Play an important role in loss-prevention and loss-reduction efforts
- Support research in the insurance mechanism

A CPCU could violate Rule R4.2 by supporting self-serving changes to the insurance mechanism that do not benefit the public or improve the insurance mechanism, or by working to prevent changes that would benefit the public interest.

People are likely to have widely varying opinions regarding the effect of proposed changes in the insurance mechanism. In fact, some CPCUs have publicly supported issues that others oppose. While not specifically mentioned in the Guidelines that relate to improving the insurance mechanism, the BEI would not become involved in an ethics action based primarily on a difference in opinion regarding some proposed change unless it were unequivocally shown that the CPCU's position is based on personal gain at the expense of the public.

Guideline G4.9 – Individual Participation in Political or Governmental Activities

The ethical obligation to strive for improvement in the functioning of the private insurance mechanism does not bar a CPCU from serving in the public sector, nor does it bar a CPCU, as an individual citizen, from supporting a governmental role in providing economic security for the citizenry. But a CPCU should be mindful of the restriction imposed by R8.4, and should avoid even the appearance of speaking on behalf of the American Institute, especially on political matters.

CPCUs are not prohibited from serving in the public sector in elected, appointed, volunteer, or advisory positions. CPCUs have served as state insurance commissioners and held other political offices, even serving as governors. By becoming involved in public-sector activities, CPCUs can play a valuable role in improving the insurance mechanism.

Politicians, regulators, lobbyists, and others in the public sector have frequently been the target of ethics violations, often arising from conflicts of interest. CPCUs engaged in public-sector activities should be especially cautious to support activities that would serve to improve the insurance mechanism and best serve the public interest, and to place the public interest above their own. Often, private interests also benefit from activities that benefit the public.

Although CPCUs are required to "support efforts" that improve insurance, these efforts are not always successful. R4.2 requires effort, not success.

CPCUs may act as individuals in "supporting a governmental role" in insurance- and risk-related activities. For example, a CPCU is not barred from writing a letter to a state representative or regulator expressing his or her views on pending legislation, provided he or she does not imply representation of other CPCUs or the American Institute.

A CPCU should use the CPCU letters after his or her name if, for instance, writing a letter to a state representative to encourage a vote against a bill, or a letter to an editor, or an article for publication. However, he or she should not imply expressing the view of other CPCUs or of the American Institute. A CPCU also may invite other CPCUs to add their signatures to a letter as long as no coercion is involved and it is clear that all CPCUs are expressing an individual opinion and not suggesting that they speak for a larger group.

Other Related Code Provisions

Striving to improve the functioning of the insurance mechanism may involve activities that seek to influence others, such as writing articles or public speaking, to which the following items relate:

- R2.1 complements R4.1 by emphasizing that keeping informed is an essential element of competence.

- G5.2 emphasizes that when writing or speaking publicly as a CPCU, a CPCU should maintain the dignity and high professional standards appropriate to the designation.

- According to G7.6, CPCUs are not required to support lobbying efforts or proposed legislation, nor are they required to take positions on controversial issues.

- G7.6 and R8.4 clarify that CPCUs may engage in lobbying activities, support proposed legislation, or take a position on controversial issues, provided that each CPCU does so as an individual and does not appear to speak on behalf of the American Institute.

Relevant Hypothetical Case Studies

The Rules under Canon 4 are considered in the following HCSs:

- HCS 103
- HCS 105
- HCS 107
- HCS 111
- HCS 112
- HCS 113
- HCS 116
- HCS 117
- HCS 118

Question to Consider

In what ways should a CPCU use his or her knowledge and skills in improving the insurance mechanism?

Suggested Answer

A CPCU should use his or her knowledge and skills to improve the insurance mechanism by improving insurance contracts, maintaining insurers' financial strength, helping ensure insurance availability, and helping reduce the cost of insurance. CPCUs can also encourage loss control and can support sound research that will lead to improvement in the insurance system.

CANON 5 – MAINTAINING AND RAISING PROFESSIONAL STANDARDS

CPCUs should assist in maintaining and raising professional standards in the insurance business.

The first three Rules under this Canon involve getting competent people into the insurance business and encouraging their growth, as well as fostering competence and ethical conduct. The last rule addresses professional standards differently. Basically, CPCUs are required to cooperate with regulatory authorities when an insurance practitioner's conduct comes into question. (The BEI is not a regulatory authority. Rule R9.2 discusses CPCUs' participation in ethics investigations by the American Institute.)

Rule R5.1 – Bring Qualified People Into the Business

A CPCU shall support personnel policies and practices that attract qualified individuals to the insurance business, provide them with ample and equal opportunities for advancement, and encourage them to aspire to the highest levels of professional competence and achievement.

Rule R5.2 – Assist Others in Pursuing CPCU and Other Studies

A CPCU shall encourage and assist qualified individuals who wish to pursue CPCU or other studies that will enhance their professional competence.

Rule R5.3 – Support Measures to Foster Competence and Ethical Conduct

A CPCU shall support the development, improvement, and enforcement of laws, regulations, and codes that will foster competence and ethical conduct on the part of all insurance practitioners and benefit the public.

Rule R5.4 – Support Regulatory Investigations

A CPCU shall not withhold information or assistance officially requested by appropriate regulatory authorities who are investigating or prosecuting any alleged violation of laws or regulations.

Guidelines

The following Guidelines discuss the application of Canon 5 and the four related Rules:

Guideline G5.1 – Setting an Example

A CPCU should assist in raising professional standards in the insurance business. Minimally, every CPCU should conduct his or her business activities in a manner that will inspire other practitioners to do likewise.

The Rules under Canon 5 emphasize other people, but also include maintaining one's own professional standards. G5.1 reminds CPCUs that they should set an example through their own professional conduct.

Guideline G5.2 – Encouraging Others' Professional Development

Both the insuring public and the insurance industry will benefit from continued growth in the number of insurance practitioners who achieve a high level of professional attainment. Thus, Rule R5.2 stipulates that "A CPCU shall encourage and assist qualified individuals who wish to pursue CPCU or other studies that will enhance their professional competence."

CPCUs are ethically obligated to encourage other qualified persons to pursue CPCU and other studies. CPCUs should offer others encouragement and information about the CPCU program.

A CPCU should share with all other insurance practitioners, as well as fellow CPCUs, the benefits of his or her professional attainments. A CPCU's conduct should be guided by a spirit of altruistic concern for the public interest. The public interest is best served when all insurance practitioners are well-informed.

CPCUs, like other professionals, should share their expertise with others. For example, many CPCUs have become CPCU/IIA course leaders; others conduct CPCU Society or other seminars, engage in research projects, write textbooks, grade exams, or serve in various volunteer roles.

A CPCU should support and participate in educational activities that assist other practitioners in their professional development. Examples of such activities include seminars, lectures, research projects, teaching, preparation of educational materials for training programs, and preparation of professional articles for publication. In writing or speaking publicly as a CPCU, however, the CPCU should maintain the dignity and high professional standards appropriate to the designation.

The authors of the Code considered obligating CPCUs to share the benefits of their professional attainments with other insurance practitioners. Some, however, felt that such a rule would obligate CPCUs to divulge trade secrets and knowledge that provide a competitive advantage. The compromise wording requires CPCUs to support efforts to improve the public understanding of insurance and risk management with the dignity associated with the CPCU tradition. Although CPCUs have an ethical obligation to share the benefits of their knowledge, a distinction exists between sharing basic knowledge and divulging trade secrets. The following clarifies this point:

This Guideline does not obligate a CPCU to divulge trade secrets or other information that would put him or her at a competitive disadvantage. Instead, it serves as a reminder that a CPCU should play a role in the development of the insurance field by sharing knowledge with other practitioners and students.

Other Related Code Provisions

Other Code provisions also relate to maintaining and raising professional standards in the insurance business, as follows:

- Supervisors and others whose occupational duties involve others' career development should consider their aspirational duties under Canon 4, as well as their obligations under the related Rules. Those in leadership positions cannot diligently perform their occupational duties unless they encourage their employees' professional development.

- G7.6 includes guidelines on lobbying or other activities in which a CPCU may engage while meeting his or her R5.3 obligations to support legislation and regulations that foster competence and ethical conduct in insurance.

- While R5.4 requires CPCUs to cooperate with investigations by regulatory authorities, R9.2 requires CPCUs to cooperate with the American Institute in any investigation of an ethics complaint.

- R5.3, R5.4, and R9.2 do not require a CPCU to report illegal or unethical behavior. In fact, R6.2 and G6.6 indicate that CPCUs should use caution and sound judgment when dealing with confidential information.

Relevant Hypothetical Case Studies

The Rules under Canon 5 are considered in the following HCSs:

- HCS 101
- HCS 111
- HCS 114

Question to Consider

Does the Code obligate a CPCU to answer all questions posed by appropriate regulatory authorities investigating other CPCUs' conduct?

Suggested Answer

Yes, the Code obligates a CPCU to answer all questions posed by appropriate regulatory authorities investigating other CPCUs' conduct.

CANON 6 – PROFESSIONAL RELATIONSHIPS

CPCUs should strive to establish and maintain dignified and honorable relationships with those whom they serve, with fellow insurance practitioners, and with members of other professions.

This Canon involves CPCUs' relationships with the following three groups of people:

1. Their customers (those whom they serve)
2. Fellow insurance practitioners
3. Members of other professions

CPCUs should strive to establish and maintain relationships that are both dignified and honorable. The insurance profession has long been characterized as a business of utmost good faith. Most insurance transactions require that a strong element of trust be part of both the image and the reality of an insurance or risk management professional.

Rule R6.1 – Legal Limitations

A CPCU shall keep informed on the legal limitations imposed on the scope of his or her professional duties.

Legal limitations depend on both the nature of the CPCU's duties and the laws that affect them. For example, claim representatives, as well as others involved in the claim process, should not engage in the unauthorized practice of law. Likewise, they should follow any unfair claim practice acts to which they are subject. Insurance advisors should not give advice that requires a securities license unless they have one. Underwriters, producers, and others are subject to unfair trade practice acts that include such sensitive topics as unfair discrimination. Licensed practitioners are subject to the regulatory provisions associated with their licenses. Whatever their professional duties, CPCUs are expected to know their legal limitations.

Rule R6.2 – Confidential Information

A CPCU shall not disclose any confidential information entrusted to, or obtained by, the CPCU in the course of his or her business or professional activities, unless a disclosure of such information is required by law or is made to a person who necessarily must have the information in order to discharge occupational or professional duties.

In the normal course of business, people in insurance and risk management have access to confidential information. Insurance files contain information on individuals' health, income, and reputation. Insurers accumulate data on businesses that include profit information, secret ingredients, business plans, products hazards, and other proprietary information and trade secrets. This information is entrusted to insurers because they need it to do business and because they implicitly agree to keep it confidential.

Rule R6.3 – Acknowledging Limitations

In rendering or proposing to render professional services for others, a CPCU shall not knowingly misrepresent or conceal any limitations on his or her ability to provide the quantity or quality of professional services the circumstances require.

Guidelines

The following Guidelines discuss the application of Canon 6 and the three related Rules.

Guideline G6.1 – Exude Competence and Ethics

By exhibiting high levels of professional competence and ethical conduct, a CPCU should constantly strive to merit the confidence and respect of those whom he or she serves, fellow practitioners, and members of other professions.

The best way to obtain and maintain a good reputation is to earn it.

Guidelines G6.2 and G6.3 – Relationships With Other Practitioners

Both G6.2 and G6.3 address relationships with other practitioners.

G6.2: A CPCU should strive to establish and maintain dignified and honorable relationships with competitors, as well as with fellow practitioners.

G6.3: A CPCU should strive to establish and maintain dignified and honorable relationships with members of other professions, including but not limited to law, medicine, and accounting. The insurance industry relies heavily on the expertise and cooperation of such professionals in fulfilling its obligation to deliver insurance benefits promptly and otherwise render high-quality insurance service to the public.

CPCUs should strive to maintain good relationships not only with their counterparts in other professions but also with their competitors and fellow practitioners, regardless of whether they are also CPCUs or CPCU candidates.

Guideline G6.4 – Independent Judgment

Like other professionals, a CPCU should maintain the knowledge and skills necessary to exercise independent judgment in the performance of his or her professional services. However, a CPCU should also be mindful of his or her personal limitations. Therefore, a CPCU should seek the counsel of other professionals, not only at the request of those whom he or she may serve but also on the CPCU's own initiative, particularly in doubtful or difficult situations or when the quality of professional service may otherwise be enhanced by such consultation.

Guideline G6.4 adds another dimension to Rule R2.1, which requires CPCUs to keep informed on technical matters that relate to their area of practice. To live up to their aspirations as professionals, CPCUs should be informed well enough to exercise independent judgment. In accordance with R6.1 and R6.3, they also should recognize their legal and professional limitations. A CPCU should be willing to get advice from other professionals, both inside and outside the insurance and risk management profession. Not only should CPCUs be willing to seek outside advice, but they should also exercise the initiative to get it when it will enable them to better serve the public.

Independent judgment is an essential characteristic of many professionals. Any person passing professional judgment on an insurance or a risk management situation should exercise independent judgment and also acknowledge any limitations, legal or otherwise, to his or her expertise.

Guideline G6.5 – Legal Limitations

A CPCU is obligated to keep fully informed on any and all legal limitations imposed on the scope of his or her professional activities. A CPCU should always exercise caution to avoid engaging in, or giving the appearance of engaging in, the unauthorized practice of law. However, a CPCU who is otherwise qualified by virtue of his or her admission to the bar may practice law.

Insurance and risk management practitioners deal with legal relationships, legal rights, and other legal and contractual—and even medical—matters. CPCUs complete a course on business law and its relation to insurance. Much of their study in other areas is also based on an understanding of related legal principles. CPCUs may answer questions that are technically legal questions as long as they do not presume to be authorities on the law. Some CPCUs, however, are also lawyers and are legally qualified to state an authoritative legal opinion.

CPCUs can easily be tempted to go beyond their authority. Because of their specialization in insurance, many CPCUs know more about certain insurance-related areas of the law than attorneys with other specialties who are authorized to render a legal opinion.

Guideline G6.6 – Sound Judgment

Beyond the obligations under Rule R6.2, a CPCU should exercise caution and sound judgment in dealing with any confidential or privileged information.

R6.2 does not prohibit CPCUs from disclosing confidential information when they are required to do so by law or when the disclosure is made to a person who must legitimately have the information to do his or her job. However, G6.6 encourages CPCUs to think and consider the consequences before sharing sensitive information. This Rule applies beyond insurance-related information or activities.

Related Code Provisions

Factors leading to dignified and honorable relationships are also mentioned in other parts of the Code, as follows:

- G6.4, suggesting that a professional should be able to exercise independent judgment, is closely related to R2.1, which requires a CPCU to keep informed on the technical matters necessary to remain professionally competent. Ideally, CPCUs should understand issues well enough to evaluate them and be able to express their own opinions.

- A violation of R3.3 can easily result from failure to keep informed of one's legal limitations, as required by R6.1.

- The Rules under Canon 8, especially those relating directly to the dignified use of the CPCU credential, are especially important in establishing dignified relationships with other professionals.

Relevant Hypothetical Case Studies

The Rules under Canon 6 are considered in the following HCSs:

- HCS 102
- HCS 103
- HCS 104
- HCS 110
- HCS 111
- HCS 117

Questions to Consider

1. CPCUs should strive to establish and maintain dignified and honorable relationships with insurance practitioners and other professionals. What is the connection between professional relationships and ethical behavior?

2. A CPCU should proudly display the CPCU designation and explain its significance. Yet, every CPCU has many limitations in his or her professional expertise. What steps should a CPCU take to compensate for these limitations?

3. Most insurance activities necessarily require the use of confidential business or personal information, such as the specific injuries of an accident victim or the earnings of a firm's individual employees. Some items of information may even be relevant to civil or criminal actions. How should a CPCU treat confidential information while remaining true to both Canons 5 and 6?

Suggested Answers

1. The connection between professional relationships and ethical behavior is that anyone who is dignified and honorable does not exceed his or her legal limitations, disclose confidential information inappropriately, or misrepresent his or her professional abilities.

2. A CPCU can compensate for his or her own limitations by acknowledging them and drawing on the knowledge of other professionals when necessary. It helps to have established a dignified and an honorable relationship with other professionals.

3. In the case of civil or criminal actions, a CPCU should not release confidential information to others unless it is required by law or required by someone to perform legitimate occupational duties.

CANON 7 – PUBLIC EDUCATION

CPCUs should assist in improving the public understanding of insurance and risk management.

Rule R7.1 restates the broad goal in the Canon somewhat more narrowly. CPCUs are not obligated to directly provide public information, but they are ethically obligated to support efforts to convey information to the public. Rule R7.2 provides the corollary—what CPCUs should not do.

Because a public understanding of insurance and risk management can lead to improvements in the insurance mechanism, Canon 7 is closely related to part of Canon 4.

Rule R7.1 – Support Efforts to Provide Information

A CPCU shall support efforts to provide members of the public with objective information concerning their risk management and insurance needs and the products, services, and techniques available to meet their needs.

Rule R7.2 – Provide Accurate Information

A CPCU shall not misrepresent the benefits, costs, or limitations of any risk management technique or any product or service of an insurer.

Guideline G7.4 – Deceptive Advertising or Business Practice

A CPCU should neither engage in nor condone deceptive advertising or business practices that significantly mislead the public or otherwise contribute to the widespread misunderstanding or misuse of insurance. All CPCU communication with the public should provide objective and factual information.

Other Guidelines

Guideline G7.1 – All CPCUs Should Improve Public Understanding

Fulfillment of all the public's insurance needs would appreciably enhance the economic and social well-being of society. But the public's insurance needs can be fully met only if every citizen recognizes his or her insurance needs and appreciates the importance of seeking competent and ethical assistance in analyzing and meeting them. This requires the combined efforts of all knowledgeable insurance professionals. Accordingly, every CPCU should assist in every practical manner to improve the public understanding of insurance and risk management, even if the CPCU does not specialize in insurance education, marketing, claim settlement, safety engineering, advertising, or other professional activities that provide frequent opportunities to communicate directly to the public.

Many CPCUs work in positions that regularly involve writing for publication, public speaking, or other types of public contact. CPCUs are not ethically required to enter into these activities. However, they are required to support them.

Though they may not be immediately obvious, CPCUs—even those who do not work in public relations, education, or other public-contact positions—have many opportunities to improve the public understanding of insurance and risk management, such as the following:

- Producers, claim representatives, and others who deal directly with the public should strive to explain insurance policies and transactions as clearly and completely as possible.

- Many CPCU chapters provide a speakers bureau service. Members are available to speak on insurance and risk management topics to outside groups. Scripts for some topics are provided by the CPCU Society.

- Many CPCU chapters support insurance education programs in local high schools and colleges. CPCUs can serve as adjunct faculty members, guest speakers, or committee members.

- Many CPCUs serve as course leaders for CPCU and IIA programs.

- CPCUs often serve as speakers and panelists for other professional organizations.

- CPCUs can make themselves available to members of the press who are looking for somebody to interview following a catastrophe or other newsworthy event.

- Many CPCU chapters engage in research projects.

- CPCUs, as individuals and in conjunction with others, write articles for the *CPCU e-Journal* and other publications. Some contribute to the public understanding by submitting letters to the editor in trade publications or newspapers.

Guidelines G7.2 and G7.3 – Remain Current in Areas of Change

G7.2 and G7.3 are closely related, as follows:

G7.2: A CPCU should keep abreast of legislation, changing conditions, and/or other developments that may affect the insuring public, and should assist in keeping the public informed of such.

G7.3: In order to contribute to a better public understanding of insurance and risk management, every CPCU should maintain and improve his or her knowledge and communication skills. However, no CPCU should hesitate to admit that he or she does not know the answer to a question. Nor should a CPCU attempt to answer such a question if it is outside the realm of his or her professional competence, authority, or proper function.

As noted in the discussion of Canon 2 and its only rule, Rule R2.1, CPCUs are ethically obligated to keep current, at least in the areas required to do their jobs. They are required by R4.2 to support improvements in the insurance mechanism. G6.4 directs CPCUs to understand the issues well enough to exercise independent judgment. G7.2 indicates that CPCUs should also aspire to keep abreast of changes that may affect the public so that they can help explain them. G7.3 emphasizes that knowledge is of limited use unless it can be communicated.

CPCU candidates are held to the same rules as CPCUs. Both candidates and CPCUs should not hesitate to admit that they do not know the answer to a question, nor should they attempt to answer a question they cannot competently address. This guideline is intended for use in practical situations.

Guideline G7.5 – Limitations of Insurance

The public should recognize its overall risk management needs and the extent to which insurance can and cannot meet them. For example, a CPCU should seize opportunities to stress the importance of loss prevention and reduction in any well-conceived risk management program.

Insurance is not always the best or most appropriate way to address some risk management needs. All CPCUs should recognize that loss control measures and alternative, noninsurance risk financing measures are appropriate and desirable components of many risk management programs.

Guideline G7.6 – Objective Public Information

Rule R7.1 stipulates that "A CPCU shall support efforts to provide members of the public with objective information concerning their risk management and insurance needs and the products, services, and techniques available to meet their needs." However, neither the Rules nor the Guidelines require a CPCU to support lobbying efforts or proposed legislation or to take positions on controversial issues. Nor do any of the Code standards prohibit a CPCU from engaging in such activities in his or her own name and as an individual. A CPCU who elects to engage in such activities should take great care to avoid violating Rule R8.4.

G7.6 answers a question that has not directly been posed: If CPCUs are ethically obligated to provide objective public information on insurance-related products that meet the public's needs, does it follow that CPCUs are ethically obligated to support legislation that would provide new insurance products?

CPCUs are not ethically required to lobby or otherwise inform the public of services that may become available if certain legislation is passed. In fact, G7.6 explicitly states that CPCUs are not ethically required to take positions on pending legislation or other controversial issues. However, they should exercise independent judgment and continually study the issues.

Although CPCUs are not required to be politically active, they are not prohibited, either. Rule R4.2 may even require taking a position on some issues that would improve the insurance mechanism. The Code prohibits CPCUs from appearing to represent the Institute. CPCUs who are members of the CPCU Society are also subject to the CPCU Society's Code of Ethics, which includes the following "specified unethical practice" in Section 4.a.5:

> To write, speak, or act in such a way as to lead another to reasonably believe that the member is officially representing the Society or a chapter of the Society unless the member has been duly authorized to do so.

The CPCU Society, not the American Institute, is responsible for enforcing the CPCU Society's Code of Ethics.

Related Code Provisions

Other portions of the Code also relate to CPCUs' activities in promoting public understanding of insurance and risk management, as follows:

- Canon 2 and R2.1 indicate the importance of continuous learning to understand the issues.
- R4.2 requires CPCUs to support efforts to improve the insurance mechanism; doing so often involves public education.
- R5.3 requires CPCUs to support certain types of laws and regulations that will benefit the public. As with R4.2, this often requires public education.
- While it is appropriate, and even desirable, for CPCUs to give visibility to their designation when speaking or writing publicly, R8.4 cautions CPCUs to avoid leaving any appearance that a CPCU is speaking on behalf of the American Institute.

Relevant Hypothetical Case Studies

The following four HCSs mention Canon 7 or related rules:

- HCS 106
- HCS 107
- HCS 109
- HCS 111

Questions to Consider

1. One way a CPCU can improve the insurance mechanism is to support proposed legislation that he or she believes is favorable and consistent with the goals of service to the public. Does the Code encourage or discourage lobbying efforts by a CPCU speaking as an individual?
2. What precautions should a CPCU take when expressing a position on political or other issues?

Suggested Answers

1. The Code neither requires nor prohibits lobbying activities. Such activities can be appropriate and desirable in improving the public understanding of insurance and risk management, as well as leading to improvement in the insurance mechanism.

2. CPCUs who lobby or otherwise take a public position on controversial issues should clarify that they are acting as individuals and not on behalf of the American Institute or the CPCU Society.

CANON 8 – INTEGRITY OF THE CPCU DESIGNATION

CPCUs should honor the integrity of the CPCU designation and respect the limitations placed on its use.

The integrity of the CPCU designation is honored when the designation and the key that symbolizes it are used in a professional, dignified manner. Rule R8.1 and the related Guidelines explicitly specify the ways in which the designation and key should be used.

The Rules and Guidelines associated with Canon 8 attempt to balance visibility and dignity. CPCUs are encouraged to display and use their designation proudly to enhance the recognition of this professional credential in the eyes of the public. However, CPCUs also are required to use the designation and the key in ways that preserve professional dignity.

CPCUs should not overstate the designation's significance or imply that those who are not CPCUs are inferior. Many qualified and well-educated insurance professionals do not hold the CPCU designation.

Rule R8.1 – Use of the CPCU Designation and Key

A CPCU shall use the CPCU designation and the CPCU key only in accordance with the relevant Guidelines promulgated by the American Institute.

This is the only Rule in the entire Code that specifically refers to the Guidelines. The Guidelines that appear in the originally published Code, as well as in the form of published Advisory Opinions, are part of this Rule. Failure to adhere to these Guidelines is a Rule violation.

The relevant Guideline is G8.1. Because of its length, commentary is interspersed throughout the Guideline.

Guideline G8.1 – Authorized Uses of the CPCU Key and Designation

Rule R8.1 of the Code of Professional Ethics stipulates that "A CPCU shall use the CPCU designation and the CPCU key only in accordance with the relevant Guidelines promulgated by the American Institute." These Guidelines, which define and impose restrictions upon the privilege to use the CPCU designation and key, are set forth subsequently. They are designed to prevent undignified commercialization of the designation, unfair comparison with able and well-established insurance practitioners who do not hold the designation, and other unethical practices inconsistent with the professional concepts that the CPCU represents. Specifically, every CPCU has an ethical obligation to comply with the following minimum standards:

a. The designation Chartered Property Casualty Underwriter, the initials CPCU, and the CPCU key may be used only in a dignified and professional manner, according to the following provisions:

1. The designation or initials may be used after the holder's name on business cards, stationery, office advertising, signed articles, business and professional listings, and telephone listings, except where such use would conflict with the provisions of subparagraph a.3.

2. The CPCU key (actual size or reduced, but not enlarged) may be imprinted only on business cards and stationery used exclusively by CPCUs. Copies of the CPCU key suitable for reproduction are available from the American Institute.

3. The designation itself, the initials CPCU, and the CPCU key are not to be used as part of a firm, partnership, or corporate name, trademark, or logo, or affixed to any object, product, or property, for any purpose whatsoever, except by the American Institute.

Different opinions may exist about what constitutes "dignified and professional." The Institute generally applies a fairly conservative standard. Any use besides those specifically authorized must first be approved by the American Institute. When in doubt, CPCUs are urged to request appropriate permission.

Camera-ready copies of the key are available to designees and CPCUs. The key's actual height is one and one-quarter of an inch. Larger reproductions are not permitted on business cards and stationery.

Because the CPCU designation is rightfully associated only with the person who has earned it, it may not appropriately be used as part of a business name or logo.

The second part of provision 3 is especially important: Except as specifically authorized in provisions 1 and 2, the CPCU initials (whether uppercase or lowercase) and the CPCU key are not to be affixed to any object except by the American Institute or with the explicit permission of the American Institute.

b. The designation Chartered Property Casualty Underwriter, the initials CPCU, and the CPCU key may be used to announce the conferment of the designation.

1. News releases prepared by the American Institute are made available to all new CPCU designees. Only these approved releases, with the addition of personal biographical information, may be used by individual CPCU designees in preparing material for the business and community press.

Approved news releases are worded to give due visibility to the accomplishment of the designee, while preserving the dignity of the CPCU designation, and to avoid any wording that might violate R8.2 or R8.3.

2. The American Institute encourages employers of new designees to publish in company publications articles congratulating the

new designees. The American Institute's official listing of new designees, published at the time of the conferment ceremony, should be used to verify the names of new designees. Copies of the CPCU key are available from the American Institute for reproduction in such articles.

3. The American Institute encourages the use of dignified advertisements congratulating new designees on earning the CPCU designation. Copies of the CPCU key are available from the American Institute for reproduction in such advertisements. These advertisements must be strictly congratulatory in nature, however, and should not include the business conducted by the firm, the lines of insurance carried by the firm, the firm's telephone number, or any copy soliciting business.

c. The designation Chartered Property Casualty Underwriter, the initials CPCU, and the CPCU key may be used by the CPCU Society in a manner that complies with the Rules and Guidelines of the American Institute's Code of Professional Ethics and that has first been authorized in writing by the Ethics Counsel of the American Institute.

The CPCU Society sells CPCU jewelry and other items bearing the CPCU designation and/or key. Items sold by the Society have been approved by the American Institute, unless they reflect the CPCU Society logo rather than the CPCU letters or key.

d. The designation Chartered Property Casualty Underwriter, the initials CPCU, and the CPCU key may not be used in any manner that violates a Rule of the Code of Professional Ethics. Rules R8.2, R8.3, and R8.4 deserve special mention in this context since they relate directly to, and impose restrictions upon, the privilege to use the CPCU designation.

e. The designation Chartered Property Casualty Underwriter, the initials CPCU, and the CPCU key may be used in any other manner that has received prior approval in writing from the Ethics Counsel of the American Institute.

Use of the CPCU designation on custom-made items of jewelry or other objects is not authorized unless it is specifically approved by the Ethics Counsel.

This Guideline has been supplemented by two Advisory Opinions. The first prohibits the use of the "CPCU" letters, by themselves or along with other letters or numbers, on license plates. Rule R8.1 incorporates by reference any guidelines published by the American Institute, and these Advisory Opinions therefore have the force of a Rule. Usage prohibited by these Advisory Opinions could lead to sanctions under the enforcement provisions of the Code. The second Advisory Opinion addresses the use of the CPCU designation and key on Web pages, as follows:

Advisory Opinion Regarding Use of the Designation Chartered Property Casualty Underwriter, the Initials CPCU, and the CPCU Key on a Web Page

The Guidelines applicable to business cards, stationery, office advertising, signed articles, business and professional listings, and telephone listings also apply to use of the designation and key on Web pages by CPCUs or organizations employing CPCUs. CPCU keys should not be enlarged, the designation should relate only to individual designation-holders (not the organization), and any explanation should not directly or indirectly overstate the designation's value. All use should be professional and dignified. CPCUs are encouraged to link their Web pages to the American Institute's Web site at www.aicpcu.org. (The CPCU Society also encourages members to link to its Web site at www.cpcusociety.org.)

The American Institute for CPCU, the CPCU Society, and CPCU Society chapters may use the designation Chartered Property Casualty Underwriter, the initials CPCU, and the CPCU key on a Web page, where they may also use the designation or initials as part of the organization name, provided the use is otherwise consistent with these guidelines.

Any questions regarding the appropriateness of existing or draft Web pages may be directed to the Ethics Counsel of the American Institute.

Advisory Opinion Regarding Use of the Initials CPCU in a Web Page Address or an E-mail Address

The initials CPCU, whether uppercase or lowercase, by themselves, or within a longer address, may not be used as part of a Web page address or an e-mail address, except by the American Institute for CPCU, the CPCU Society, and CPCU Society chapters.

Advisory Opinion Regarding Use of the Initials CPCU in a Telephone Number

The initials CPCU, whether uppercase or lowercase, should not be used as part of a telephone number in advertisements, publications, or other listings except by the American Institute for CPCU, the CPCU Society, and CPCU Society chapters.

Rule R8.2 – Overstating CPCU

A CPCU shall not attribute to the mere possession of the designation depth or scope of knowledge, skills, and professional capabilities greater than those demonstrated by successful completion of the CPCU program.

Guideline G8.2 elaborates on the intent of this Rule.

Guideline G8.2 – Misrepresentation

Rule R8.2 stipulates that "A CPCU shall not attribute to the mere possession of the designation depth or scope of knowledge, skills, and professional capabilities greater than those demonstrated by successful completion of the CPCU program." Unless this Rule is strictly observed by all CPCUs, the public will be misled and the integrity of the designation, as well as the integrity of the violator, will be significantly diminished. The public is protected and the integrity of the designation and its holder are best preserved by avoiding any misrepresentations of the nature and significance of the CPCU designation.

Rule R8.3 – Comparison With Non-CPCUs

A CPCU shall not make unfair comparisons between a person who holds the CPCU designation and one who does not.

Rule R8.4 – Acting as a Representative of the American Institute

A CPCU shall not write, speak, or act in a way that leads another to reasonably believe the CPCU is officially representing the American Institute, unless the CPCU has been authorized to do so by the American Institute.

The vast majority of CPCUs are not official representatives of the American Institute, and they should not imply that they speak for the American Institute. Normally, the only people who have the authority to speak on the American Institute's behalf are the officers and staff of the American Institute, as well as members of the American Institute's Board of Trustees.

The issue of acting as a representative of the Institute could arise in connection with local CPCU conferment ceremonies. Many CPCU chapters conduct an annual graduation ceremony in which they honor the current year's CPCU designees, following procedures specifically established by the American Institute. These procedures specify who is entitled to act as a representative of the American Institute in conducting these local ceremonies. The American Institute works with the CPCU Society to ensure an appropriate representative is available.

The Code includes Rules that the Institute's graduates and students must follow to avoid sanctions, but it does not address standards of conduct for CPCU Society members in their role as members. The Code does not address whether it is appropriate for CPCUs to speak on behalf of the CPCU Society. These issues are addressed in the CPCU Society's Code of Ethics.

Other Related Code Provisions

- Most other Code provisions allude to situations in which CPCUs use their designation as a credential to enhance their credibility and to give visibility to the CPCU movement, whether dealing with customers, the general public, or other insurance and noninsurance professionals.

- While R8.1 deals with the appropriate use of the designation, Rule R9.3 addresses unauthorized use of the CPCU designation by an individual who is not a CPCU. CPCUs are ethically obligated to report such incidents.

Relevant Hypothetical Case Studies

The Rules under Canon 8 are considered in the following HCSs:

- HCS 108
- HCS 120
- HCS121

Questions to Consider

1. How may Rule R8.4 be violated by a CPCU who is engaged in lobbying efforts?

2. In what ways does Canon 8 seek to maintain the dignity of the CPCU professional designation?

3. The Code includes specific restrictions on the ways in which the CPCU designation and the CPCU key are to be used:

    (a) What problems are these restrictions designed to prevent?

    (b) List the specific ways described in the Code in which the initials CPCU and the CPCU key may be used.

    (c) List the specific prohibitions against misuse of the CPCU designation or the CPCU key.

4. What are appropriate ways of announcing that a CPCU candidate has met all requirements and has earned and received the CPCU professional designation?

Suggested Answers

1. A CPCU engaged in lobbying efforts may violate Rule R8.4 by creating the impression that he or she is acting as a representative of the American Institute for CPCU.

2. Canon 8 seeks to maintain the dignity of the CPCU professional designation by ensuring appropriate and dignified use of the designation and the key.

3. (a) These restrictions are designed to prevent undignified commercialization and unfair comparisons, as well as any other unethical practices.

   (b) The initials CPCU and the CPCU key may be used in business cards, stationery, office advertising, signed articles, business and professional listings, telephone listings, and in any other manner approved by the American Institute for CPCU.

   (c) The CPCU designation should be treated as a personal designation that is associated with the individual CPCU. It should not be used as part of a firm, partnership, or corporate name; trademark, or logo. It should not be affixed to any object, product, or property without permission from the American Institute. The letters CPCU should not appear on a vanity license plate, a Web page address, an e-mail address, or a telephone "number" that is represented by letters.

4. Appropriate ways of announcing that a CPCU candidate has met all requirements and has earned and received the CPCU professional designation are the news release available from the American Institute, articles in an employer's publications, and dignified advertisements.

CANON 9 – INTEGRITY OF THE CODE

CPCUs should assist in maintaining the integrity of the Code of Professional Ethics.

Canons 8 and 9 concern integrity. While Canon 8 addresses the integrity of the CPCU designation, Canon 9 deals with the integrity of the Code. Like any code of ethics, the Code has integrity only if those who are bound by it consider it important and adhere to it. To maintain its integrity, the Code must also be enforced, and sanctions must be imposed on those who violate its Rules.

CPCUs support the Code's integrity by supporting only candidates who meet the ethical standards of the Code and by assisting the American Institute in enforcing the Code. CPCUs are also required to report any use of the CPCU designation by someone who is not authorized to do so.

Rule R9.1 – Supporting Candidates Who Meet Ethical Standards

A CPCU shall not initiate or support the CPCU candidacy of any individual he or she knows engages in business practices that violate the ethical standards prescribed by this Code.

This Rule stands as a complement to Rule R5.2: "A CPCU shall encourage and assist qualified individuals who wish to pursue CPCU…." While encouraging qualified individuals, CPCUs should neither initiate nor support the candidacy of any individual who engages in unethical business practices. Unethical business practices are those that violate the Code's standards. Note that R9.1 refers not to the Rules of the Code but rather to "the ethical standards prescribed by this Code." CPCUs are to initiate and support only those CPCU candidates with the high ethical standards reflected not only in the Rules but also in the Canons.

Guideline G9.1 – Maintaining Standards

A CPCU should assist in upholding the experience, educational, and ethical standards prescribed for prospective CPCU designees by the American Institute.

The goal of the American Institute and CPCUs is to raise professional standards in property and liability insurance. CPCUs should identify insurance and risk management practitioners who would make good CPCUs, recruit them as CPCU candidates, and encourage and support their candidacy.

Rule R9.2 – Reporting Violations

A CPCU possessing unprivileged information concerning an alleged violation of this Code shall, upon request, reveal such information to the

tribunal or other authority empowered by the American Institute to investigate or act upon the alleged violation.

Guidelines G9.2 and G9.3 relate primarily to this Rule.

Guideline G9.2 – Reporting Adverse Information

A CPCU should assist the American Institute in preserving the integrity of the Code, first and foremost, by voluntarily complying with both the letter and the spirit of the Code. Ultimately, however, the public can be protected and the integrity of the Code can be maintained only if the Code is strictly but fairly enforced, and this, in turn, can be achieved only if Code violations are promptly brought to the attention of the proper officials. Although a CPCU should not become a self-appointed investigator or judge on matters properly left to the BEI, every CPCU should comply with the mandates of Rules R9.1, R9.2, and R9.3. Except for the comparatively rare but troublesome situation covered by R9.3, whether a CPCU should volunteer adverse information is left to the CPCU's judgment.

Some professions have ethics rules that effectively prohibit one member from criticizing another member of the profession. The authors of the Code believed such provisions are contrary to the public interest. The Code does, however, forbid a CPCU from initiating or supporting the CPCU candidacy of a person known to engage in practices that violate the Code. It obligates a CPCU to furnish information when officially requested to do so by the Ethics Counsel. It also obligates a CPCU to report promptly to the Institute an unauthorized person's use of the CPCU designation.

CPCUs are encouraged to report Code violations so that the Code can be enforced and its integrity maintained. None of the Rules require a CPCU to report a Code violation by another CPCU or CPCU candidate. G9.2 clarifies a CPCU must use his or her judgment to decide whether to report on another CPCU. However, a CPCU violates R1.2 if he or she advocates, sanctions, participates in, or even condones a Rule violation by another CPCU or by someone who is not a CPCU. CPCUs should also recognize that they can best preserve the Code's integrity by taking steps that will lead to sanctions against those who violate it.

Canon 9 should inspire CPCUs to report Code violations, but no Rule specifically requires it. However, in deciding not to report another CPCU's violations, a CPCU should be sure he or she does not violate R1.2 by condoning the violation.

Guideline G9.3 – Committee Service

Upon request, a CPCU should serve on committees, boards, or tribunals prescribed by the American Institute for the administration or enforcement of the Code. A CPCU is obligated to disqualify himself or herself from such service if the CPCU believes, in good conscience, that he or she could not serve in a fair and an impartial manner or upon request.

A CPCU who serves as a member of the BEI or Ethics Policy Committee of the Board of Trustees should disengage himself or herself from matters in which he or she has a personal interest, or in any other case in which professional judgment suggests that he or she could not be objective.

Rule R9.3 – Reporting Unauthorized Use of the Designation

A CPCU shall report promptly to the American Institute any information concerning the use of the CPCU designation by an unauthorized person.

CPCUs are ethically required under the Code to report any use of the CPCU designation by someone who is not entitled to do so.

Only CPCUs and matriculated CPCU candidates are bound by the Code of Professional Ethics and subject to its sanctions. Persons who do not fall into these categories cannot be sanctioned by the BEI. They can, however, violate the law in misappropriating the CPCU designation, which has been trademarked by the American Institute. The Institute's General Counsel will vigorously enforce the Institute's trademark rights under civil law.

CPCU candidates who use the CPCU designation before they are entitled to do so, or without meeting all requirements of the CPCU program, may be sanctioned under the Code. Penalties may include suspending their rights to complete the program.

CPCU candidates who have taken all necessary exams are not authorized to use the CPCU designation until the date they are specifically authorized by the American Institute to do so.

Until they officially become CPCUs, CPCU candidates are not to wear the CPCU key or other CPCU jewelry, use the CPCU designation after their name, or use business cards or stationery bearing the designation. It is acceptable, however, to order CPCU jewelry and stationery so that it is available for use as soon as it becomes appropriate.

Other Related Code Provisions

- R5.2 requires CPCUs to encourage and assist qualified individuals in pursuing CPCU studies, while R9.1 clarifies that CPCUs should not support candidates whose business practices violate the Code's ethical standards.
- R6.2 requires CPCUs not to disclose confidential information unless required by law or the disclosure is made to a person who must have the information in order to discharge "legitimate occupational or professional duties." G9.2 clarifies that reporting code violations is encouraged, but not mandatory, to preserve the Code's integrity. Enforcing the Code is a "legitimate professional duty."

Relevant Hypothetical Case Studies

The following two HCSs involve Canon 9 and related Rules:

* HCS 101
* HCS 104

Questions to Consider

1. Under what circumstances should a CPCU reveal information regarding a Code violator?
2. Is a CPCU obligated to report a non-CPCU who uses the CPCU designation?

Suggested Answers

1. Except for unauthorized use of the CPCU designation, CPCUs are never required to report violations of the Code by CPCUs or CPCU candidates. However, they are ethically required to furnish information to the Ethics Counsel or other appropriate authority investigating a Code violation.
2. CPCUs are obligated to report the use of the CPCU designation by any non-CPCU, including CPCU candidates.

CHAPTER NOTE

1.   *Webster's New World Dictionary* Third College Edition, s.v. "altruism."

Disciplinary Rules, Procedures, and Penalties for the Enforcement of the Code of Professional Ethics of the American Institute for CPCU

CHAPTER 4

This chapter contains the Disciplinary Rules, Procedures, and Penalties for enforcement of the Code of Professional Ethics of the American Institute for CPCU as they appeared after the Board of Trustees of the American Institute approved the most recent amendments to them in April 1999.

I. Applicability

    A. In accordance with Articles I and IV of the Bylaws of the American Institute, the Board of Trustees has established educational, experience, and ethics standards that must be met by every individual who seeks the privilege of being designated a Chartered Property Casualty Underwriter (CPCU). The ethical standards are set forth explicitly in the Code of Professional Ethics.

       The Code consists of two kinds of standards, Canons and Rules of Professional Conduct. Whereas the Canons are general standards of an aspirational and inspirational nature, the Rules are specific standards of a mandatory and an enforceable nature. The Rules prescribe the absolute minimum level of ethical conduct required of every individual subject to the Code.

    B. Pursuant to the agreements stipulated in the application for admission to CPCU candidacy, all CPCU candidates voluntarily agree to be judged by the ethics standards prescribed by the Board of Trustees. Thus, at the time they matriculate with the American Institute and thereafter for as long as they remain candidates, all CPCU candidates are subject to the binding effect of the Rules of Professional Conduct.

    C. The Rules of Professional Conduct are also enforceable and binding upon all CPCUs whose designations are conferred after July 1976. However, by resolution of the Board of Trustees, the earliest enforcement date shall be deferred for such CPCUs until 1 July 1977.

    D. As respects CPCUs whose designations were conferred prior to July 1976, the earliest enforcement date shall be deferred until the first day following the filing, if any, of an individual CPCU's voluntary written election to be bound by the Rules of Professional Conduct or, if later, 1 July 1977.

II. Jurisdiction

    A. The investigation of an alleged violation of the Code of Professional Ethics shall be carried out by a person or persons designated by the Chairman of the Board of Ethical Inquiry.

B. As authorized by the Bylaws, adjudication of alleged violations of the Rules of Professional Conduct shall be by the Board of Ethical Inquiry and the Ethics Policy Committee.

III. Ethics Policy Committee, Board of Ethical Inquiry, Ethics Counsel

A. *Ethics Policy Committee of the Board of Trustees.* The Board of Trustees of the American Institute shall select from its members an Ethics Policy Committee. The President shall designate one of the elected members as Chairman of this committee. The Ethics Policy Committee shall have responsibility for reviewing matters of policy associated with all Institute ethics activities, making recommendations to the Executive Committee and the Board of Trustees, and providing for liaison with the CPCU Society on ethical policy considerations. The Ethics Policy Committee shall promulgate the specific disciplinary procedures and penalties to be used in enforcing the Code of Professional Ethics of the American Institute and shall have the authority to approve such periodic changes in the disciplinary procedures and penalties as may be necessary or desirable.

The Ethics Policy Committee shall also have the authority to act on behalf of the Board of Trustees on all recommendations of the Board of Ethical Inquiry concerning disciplinary matters. All revocations and suspensions of the privilege to use the CPCU designation shall be reported in writing to the Board.

B. *Board of Ethical Inquiry.* The Board of Ethical Inquiry shall consist of eight (8) members appointed by the President of the American Institute subject to the advice and consent of the Ethics Policy Committee. All members shall be CPCUs, and together they shall constitute, as nearly as is practical, a representative cross section of the occupational backgrounds and other pertinent characteristics of all CPCUs. One member shall be the Ethics Counsel, a staff officer of the American Institute other than the President, who shall serve ex officio as nonvoting chairperson. The other seven (7) members shall not be full-time employees of the American Institute or the CPCU Society.

Voting members of the Board of Ethical Inquiry shall be appointed for a term of three years, with the possibility of appointment for a second term of three years, after which members are not eligible for any additional appointment. The terms of voting members shall commence on the first day of January, and four members shall constitute a quorum.

The Board of Ethical Inquiry shall be responsible for implementing established and approved ethics policy. The principal functions of the Board of Ethical Inquiry shall be to certify that CPCU candidates have met all ethics requirements, issue opinions to CPCUs and CPCU candidates who request assistance in interpreting or applying the Code of Professional Ethics, instigate independent investigations of the facts in cases involving alleged Rule violations under the Code, and serve as the tribunal to hear and decide cases involving alleged Rule violations.

The Board of Ethical Inquiry shall, when it deems appropriate, (1) promulgate and publish guidelines to supplement the Code of Professional Ethics; (2) summarize and publish the rulings of the tribunal in cases brought before it; (3) recommend amendments and additions to the Code, improvements in the disciplinary and enforcement procedures, and changes in ethics policy; and (4) engage in such other activities that will assist in the implementation of approved ethics policies. The Board of Ethical Inquiry may carry out some of its functions through Institute staff, consultants, investigators, or subcommittees, but all disciplinary actions and published materials must be approved by a majority of its voting members. The Chairperson of the Board of Ethical Inquiry shall be the Ethics Counsel of the American Institute, who shall be the administrative head of the Board and shall preside at all meetings of the Board, but the chairperson may not participate in the deliberations of the Board in its capacity as a disciplinary tribunal.

C. *Ethics Counsel.* Ethics Counsel, hereinafter referred to as Counsel, in addition to the duties described in III. B. above, shall have the power and duty to

(1) investigate all matters involving an alleged violation of the Code;

(2) dispose of all matters (subject to the provisions of IV. B. and C.) either by dismissal or the prosecution of formal charges before a Hearing Panel or the Ethics Policy Committee of the Board of Trustees;

(3) appear at hearings conducted with respect to petitions for reinstatement by CPCUs whose designations have been suspended or revoked; cross-examine witnesses testifying in support of the motion and marshal available evidence, if any, in opposition thereto; and

(4) maintain permanent records of all ethics matters processed and the disposition thereof.

IV. Procedures

A. *Complaints.*

(1) All complaints alleging a violation of the Code of Professional Ethics shall be submitted in writing to Counsel and signed by the complainant.

(2) If, after the investigation described in paragraph B., it is decided to proceed with formal disciplinary proceedings, a copy of the complaint shall be furnished by Counsel to the person or persons against whom the complaint is lodged.

(3) Counsel, in accordance with procedures specified below, shall determine whether the complaint is of sufficient merit to warrant submission to the Board of Ethical Inquiry.

B. *Procedures Concerning Alleged Violation of the Code by CPCUs.*

(1) *Investigation.* All investigations, whether upon complaint or otherwise, shall be initiated and conducted by Counsel. Upon the conclusion of an investigation, Counsel may dismiss complaints that, in Counsel's opinion, are frivolous, prima facie without merit, or for the lack of jurisdiction. The dismissal of any other complaint by Counsel may be effected only after Counsel has secured the concurrence of two voting members of the Board of Ethical Inquiry. Counsel shall submit to the Hearing Panel of the Board of Ethical Inquiry all other complaints that are not dismissed for the reasons contained herein.

(2) *Formal Hearing.* Formal disciplinary proceedings before a Hearing Panel of the Board of Ethical Inquiry shall be commenced by setting forth the specific charges of misconduct. A copy of such charges shall be served on the respondent and/or the respondent's attorney. In the event the respondent fails to file an answer within thirty days after service of the charges, it shall be assumed that the respondent does not intend to contest the charge, and the Hearing Panel shall make its decision based solely on the evidence submitted by Counsel. If the respondent files an answer and requests the opportunity to be heard in person, Counsel, after consultation with the Hearing Panel, shall fix the date and place of a hearing, giving the respondent at least fifteen days' notice thereof. The notice of hearing shall advise the respondent that the respondent is entitled to be represented by counsel, and to present evidence in his or her own behalf. Unless the opportunity to appear personally is specifically requested by the respondent or Counsel, there shall be no formal hearing held, and the complaint, defense, and any evidence ("the record") shall be submitted by Counsel to the Hearing Panel by mail. The members of the Hearing Panel may consider the matter by means of personal conference, correspondence, telephone, or other means of communication.

The Hearing Panel shall consist of three voting members of the Board of Ethical Inquiry selected by Counsel, one of whom shall be selected by Counsel to serve as Chairperson. In selecting the members of such a Hearing Panel, Counsel shall be guided by (1) the geographical proximity of the residence of a member to the residence of the respondent and (2) the availability of such member for service. A member so selected shall disclose any fact or circumstance causing him or her to believe that, for a conflict of interests or other meritorious reason, he or she should be disqualified from serving on such Panel. Within thirty days after the conclusion of the hearing, the Hearing Panel shall submit its report to the entire Board of Ethical Inquiry. The report shall summarize the evidence and contain the recommendations of its majority and any minority opinion. The majority vote of all voting members of the Board of Ethical Inquiry voting shall determine the acceptance or rejection of the recommendation of the Hearing Panel.

In those disciplinary matters that must be reviewed by, or which are appealed to, the Ethics Policy Committee ("the Committee"), Counsel shall submit the record, including the decision of the Board of Ethical Inquiry, to the Chairperson of the Committee by mail. The respondent will be conclusively deemed to have waived all objections to the findings and recommendations of the Board of Ethical Inquiry unless the respondent had filed an answer upon service of the initial charges and notice of the institution of formal disciplinary proceedings before a Hearing Panel of the Board of Ethical Inquiry, as provided above. There shall be no formal hearing, and the Committee may make its decision on the record by means of personal conference, correspondence, telephone, or other means of communication.

The Committee shall either approve, disapprove, or modify the recommendation of the Board of Ethical Inquiry within thirty days after the submission of the record by Counsel.

(3) A CPCU convicted by verdict, guilty plea, or plea of nolo contendere of any crime that violates the Rules of Professional Conduct immediately loses the right to use the CPCU designation. Such suspension of the right to use the CPCU designation shall last indefinitely, or until the convicted party petitions the Board of Ethical Inquiry and convinces the Board of that party's fitness again to use the designation.

C. *Procedure for Disciplinary Proceedings Involving Applicants for the CPCU Program.* Whenever Counsel determines that an applicant for the CPCU program may have violated the Code of Professional Ethics, Counsel shall recommend, after investigation and in accord with the procedures herein, whether or not such applicant shall be approved or rejected.

(1) In cases where the alleged Code violation involves the breach of Rule R3.3 of the Code or the suspension of a business or professional license, but where it appears that the applicant has been fully rehabilitated, Counsel shall secure the concurrence of two members of the Board of Ethical Inquiry before Counsel may authorize the acceptance of such application. If either of such members disagrees with Counsel's recommendation, the matter shall be submitted to a Hearing Panel in the same manner as a disciplinary matter referred to in IV. B. above.

(2) If the disciplinary matter involves an alleged Code violation other than the types described in IV. C. (1) above, and where Counsel, after investigation, determines that the applicant has been fully rehabilitated, counsel shall secure the concurrence of two CPCU members of the Executive Council of the American Institute for Chartered Property Casualty Underwriters before Counsel may authorize the acceptance of such application. If either of such members disagrees with Counsel's recommendation, the matter shall be submitted to a Hearing Panel in the same manner as a disciplinary matter referred to in IV. B. above.

(3) If, after investigation, Counsel determines that the application should be rejected, Counsel shall advise the applicant in writing that the application will be submitted to a Hearing Panel of the Board of Ethical Inquiry with the recommendation that it be rejected. If the applicant contests the proposed recommendation, the applicant shall notify Counsel in writing, within thirty days of the receipt of such notice, of the desire to contest the recommendation together with any defense or evidence on the applicant's behalf. Counsel shall then submit the matter to a Hearing Panel in the same manner as a disciplinary matter referred to in IV. B. above. Unless the opportunity to appear personally is specifically requested by the respondent or Counsel, there shall be no formal hearing held, and the complaint, defense, and any evidence ("the record") shall be submitted by Counsel to the Hearing Panel by mail. The members of the Hearing Panel may consider the matter by means of personal conference, correspondence, telephone, or other means of communication. Within thirty days after the conclusion of the hearing, the Hearing Panel shall submit its report to the entire Board of Ethical Inquiry. The report shall summarize the evidence and contain the recommendation of its majority and any minority opinion.

(4) If the decision of the majority of the Board of Ethical Inquiry is to reject the application, the applicant shall have thirty (30) days within which to request a review of the decision by the Ethics Policy Committee, such review to be considered in the same manner as disciplinary matters referred to in IV. B. (2) above.

D. *Procedure for Disciplinary Proceedings Involving Candidates for the CPCU Program.* Whenever Counsel determines that a candidate for the CPCU program may have violated the Code of Professional Ethics, Counsel shall recommend, after investigation and in accord with the procedures herein, whether or not such candidate shall be approved or disapproved.

(1) In cases where the alleged Code violation involves the breach of Rule R3.3 of the Code or the suspension of a business or professional license, but where it appears that the candidate has

been fully rehabilitated, Counsel shall secure the concurrence of two members of the Board of Ethical Inquiry in the continuation of the candidacy in good standing of such candidate. If either of such members disagrees with Counsel's recommendation, the matter shall be submitted to a Hearing Panel in the same manner as a disciplinary matter referred to in IV. B. above.

(2) If the disciplinary matter involves an alleged Code violation other than the types described in IV. D. (1) above, and where Counsel, after investigation, determines that the candidate has been fully rehabilitated, Counsel shall secure the concurrence of two members of the Executive Council of the American Institute for Chartered Property Casualty Underwriters in continuation of the candidacy in good standing of such candidate. If either of such members disagrees with Counsel's recommendation, the matter will be submitted to a Hearing Panel in the same manner as a disciplinary matter referred to in IV. B. above.

(3) If, after investigation, Counsel determines that the candidacy in good standing of such candidate should be terminated, Counsel shall advise the candidate in writing that the matter will be submitted to a Hearing Panel of the Board of Ethical Inquiry with the recommendation to terminate the candidacy.

If the candidate contests the proposed recommendation, the candidate shall notify Counsel in writing, within thirty days of the receipt of such notice, of the desire to contest the recommendation together with any defense or evidence on the candidate's behalf. Counsel shall then submit the matter to a Hearing Panel in the same manner as a disciplinary matter referred to in IV. B. above. Unless the opportunity to appear personally is specifically requested by the respondent or Counsel, there shall be no formal hearing held, and the complaint, defense, and any evidence ("the record") shall be submitted by Counsel to the Hearing Panel by mail. The members of the Hearing Panel may consider the matter by means of personal conference, correspondence, telephone, or other means of communication. Within thirty days after the conclusion of the hearing, the Hearing Panel shall submit its report to the entire Board of Ethical Inquiry. The report shall summarize the evidence and contain the recommendation of its majority and any minority opinion.

(4) If the majority of the Board of Ethical Inquiry rejects the application, the candidate shall have thirty (30) days within which to request a review of the decision by the Ethics Policy Committee. Such review would be considered in the same manner as disciplinary matters referred to in IV. B. (2) above.

(5) A candidate convicted by verdict, guilty plea, or plea of nolo contendere of any crime that violates the Rules of Professional

Conduct is immediately suspended from further participation in the CPCU program. Such suspension shall last indefinitely, or until the convicted party petitions the Board of Ethical Inquiry and convinces the Board of that party's fitness again to participate in the CPCU program.

V. **Penalties**

A. If the Board of Ethical Inquiry determines that a complaint merits disciplinary action, it may impose or recommend, as appropriate, any penalty hereinafter described, provided that the severity of the penalty imposed shall be commensurate with the severity of the offense committed. The Board of Ethical Inquiry may also consider all the circumstances surrounding the commission of any offense and the likelihood that the offender has been rehabilitated. All penalties recommended by the Board of Ethical Inquiry must be reviewed, before becoming effective, by the Ethics Policy Committee and approved or modified as appropriate.

B. Penalties that may be administered in appropriate cases are as follows:

(1) with respect to CPCUs subject to the Code:

(a) private admonitions, requesting the violator to cease and desist;

(b) reprimands in the form of informal rebukes given limited publication;

(c) censures in the form of formal rebukes given wide publication; and Disciplinary Rules, Procedures, and Penalties; and

(d) revocation or suspension of the privilege to use the CPCU designation, for a probationary period or indefinitely, with or without publication.

(2) with respect to CPCU applicants and candidates, admission to any examination may be denied, and awarding of the CPCU designation may be withheld pending receipt of convincing proof of the candidate's full and complete rehabilitation.

C. All proceedings involving allegations of breach of the Rules of Professional Conduct shall be kept confidential except as to the parties, but penalties assessed and decisions made may be disclosed, provided the publication of disciplinary sanctions to others shall be approved by the Ethics Policy Committee.

VI. **Miscellaneous Provisions**

A. (1) Complaints against members of the Board of Ethical Inquiry or Counsel involving alleged violation of the Rules of Professional Conduct by them shall be submitted directly to the Ethics Policy Committee.

(2) Complaints against members of the Ethics Policy Committee involving alleged violations of the Rules of Professional Conduct by them shall be submitted directly to the Board of Trustees of the American Institute for Chartered Property Casualty Underwriters.

B. Amendments to these Disciplinary Rules, Procedures, and Penalties shall bear their effective date as determined by the Ethics Policy Committee.

Effective 31 August 1976, as amended 17 June 1983, 12 June 1984, 16 February 1990, 16 June 1995, and 14 April 1999

Edwin S. Overman, PhD, CPCU

Chairman

Ethics Policy Committee

Hypothetical Case Studies of the Board of Ethical Inquiry

One of the most important functions of the Board of Ethical Inquiry (BEI) is to facilitate voluntary compliance with the standards established by the Code of Professional Ethics (the Code). Accordingly, the BEI periodically publishes Guidelines and Advisory Opinions (Opinions). Whenever questions of interpretation arise, CPCUs and CPCU candidates are encouraged to request Advisory Opinions. Only the BEI is authorized to issue such opinions on behalf of the American Institute.

Unpublished Opinions are informal and intended solely for the guidance of the individuals to whom they are issued; published Opinions are formal and intended for everyone subject to the Code. Published Opinions are presented as BEI responses to Hypothetical Case Studies (HCSs).

The cases and their corresponding Opinions, which are designated by the initials "HCS" and numbered, did not arise from actual disciplinary proceedings. The cases' hypothetical nature preserves the anonymity of inquirers and provides an efficient means of posing a wide variety of ethical questions and issues to which the Code may be applied. The BEI's Opinions anticipate and resolve such questions and issues in advance.

Published Opinions may differ appreciably from the decisions rendered in actual disciplinary proceedings. Nonetheless, as official interpretations and applications of the Rules, the Opinions offer guidance for CPCUs and CPCU candidates.

CASE HCS-101—Ethics and Legal Violations Before Matriculation

Richard Roe, when completing his matriculation application for the CPCU program, provided complete information regarding his past record of criminal convictions. Further investigation confirmed that he received his high school diploma in 1982 while confined to a juvenile correctional institution for several counts of shoplifting, disorderly conduct, assault, and resisting arrest. Within six weeks after his probationary release from the juvenile institution, Roe was arrested and charged with armed robbery. He was convicted and served ten years in prison.

In 1992, the personnel director of an insurance company hired Roe to work in the company's printing shop. Seven years later, Roe, having successfully completed the Insurance Institute of America Program in General Insurance, was promoted to the position of underwriting trainee. He has since advanced to the position of junior underwriter to the special risks department and has been promised another promotion if he is able to fulfill the CPCU designation requirements.

The personnel director, a CPCU, indicates that he would support Roe's candidacy. Roe, 44, is married, has two children, coaches a youth baseball team, and spends two Saturdays each month doing volunteer work. Should Roe's application for the CPCU program be approved? Did the personnel director violate the Code? Suppose Roe had not revealed his criminal record when he matriculated, but the American Institute discovered the facts after Roe passed all the required exams and met the experience requirements before the national conferment ceremonies. Should Roe receive the CPCU designation?

OPINION HCS-101—Ethics and Legal Violations Before Matriculation

The standards most directly applicable to this case are Rules R3.3 and R9.1, and Guideline G3.4.

The agreements an individual must sign at matriculation specify:

> ...all CPCU candidates become subject to the binding effect of the Rules at the time they matriculate with the American Institute, and thereafter for as long as they remain candidates.

Roe violated the spirit of Canon 3 and G3.4 on numerous occasions, both by violating laws and by engaging in activity that caused unjust harm to others. Because no disciplinary action can be taken against any person not subject to the Code, and in the absence of a Rule violation, the BEI must determine whether Roe violated R3.3. Based on the nature and number of crimes committed, the BEI believes that Roe violated R3.3 and is subject to disciplinary action.

However, the BEI could vote to admit Roe to CPCU candidacy. The Disciplinary Rules and Procedures provide that such action may be taken "where it appears that the candidate has been fully rehabilitated." The evidence presented in this case, though limited, indicates that Roe has been fully rehabilitated.

Had Roe misrepresented the facts about his criminal record, and had the American Institute discovered the misrepresentation before the designation was conferred, the BEI would withhold the designation because the misrepresentation would be a violation of R3.1 and evidence that he was not fully rehabilitated. Roe would subsequently be given an opportunity to prove his full rehabilitation. Had Roe already received the designation when the misrepresentation was discovered, the BEI would recommend to the Ethics Policy Committee that Roe's designation be suspended.

The BEI believes the personnel director did not violate R9.1. He did initiate and support Roe's CPCU candidacy, but he had no reason to suspect Roe to engage in (at the present time) business practices that violate the Code. The personnel director observed the spirit of G9.2 when he avoided becoming a "self-appointed investigator or judge on matters properly left to the BEI" and by advising Roe to disclose his criminal record. Additionally, the personnel director seemed to be complying fully with R5.1 in the spirit of Canon 1.

CASE HCS-102—Alleged Ethics Violation for CPCU Candidate

J. B. White, CPCU, is regional claims manager for a large liability insurer. After reviewing a property damage liability claim, White agrees with the adjuster that the claimant is justifiably entitled to a settlement of $3,000. However, White instructs the adjuster to offer her $1,800 and a box of good chocolates. "If the claimant refuses," White says, "explain to her that if she hires an attorney, his fee will be up to 50 percent of the settlement amount, so if she takes our offer she will be $300 ahead of the game. If she still refuses, put the file in your desk drawer for a couple of months. She will eventually see it our way because she really needs the money."

The claimant later writes to the BEI and argues that White and the adjuster are guilty of ethics violations. The adjuster says he was just following the orders of his superior. White says his action was "in accord with customary industry practices," and he "did not understand" the Rule, though he had "glanced at the Institute's Code of Professional Ethics several times." The adjuster is not yet a CPCU, but he has matriculated and passed two of the CPCU examinations.

OPINION HCS-102—Alleged Ethics Violation for CPCU Candidate

The standards most directly applicable to this case are those in Rules R1.1, R1.2, R2.1, R3.1, R3.3, and R6.1; Guidelines G1.1, G1.2, G1.3, G1.4, and G3.4; and Canons 1, 3, and 6.

Here, as elsewhere, the BEI may take or recommend disciplinary action only if the accused is subject to the binding effect of the Rules and guilty of a Rule violation. As a CPCU candidate, the adjuster is clearly bound by the Rules.

Whether White is bound by the Rules depends on when his CPCU designation was conferred. He is bound by them automatically if his designation was conferred after July 1976. But if his designation was conferred before July 1976, he is subject to the possibility of disciplinary action only if he elected to be bound unconditionally by the mandates of the Rules. For the purposes of this case, the BEI assumes that White is subject to disciplinary action.

The BEI believes that both White and the adjuster violated several Rules. In jurisdictions that have unfair claims practices acts, the liability claims settlement approach of White and the adjuster may be contrary to statute and/or regulation, in which case it would likewise violate R3.3. Neither White nor the adjuster would be allowed to plead ignorance of such laws, for the reasons explained in Guideline G3.4, because the information about such laws is readily available. Moreover, Rule R6.1 obligates them to "keep informed on the legal limitations imposed on the scope of [their] professional duties." If White and the adjuster were not aware of an applicable law governing claims representatives' conduct, then they are also in violation of the minimum continuing education obligation, which is stipulated in R2.1 and further clarified in Guidelines G2.1 through G2.4.

Regardless of whether White and the adjuster violated a statute or regulation, the BEI believes that they did violate R3.1. The claims settlement approach in question may not meet all the narrow legal tests for fraud per se, but the approach is an act of a dishonest and deceitful nature within the intended meaning of the Code provisions. Tactics of delay, bribery, and deliberate underpayment are contrary to the letter of G1.4, cause "unjust harm to others" within the meaning of Canon 3, are contrary to the Canon 6 concept of establishing and maintaining "dignified and honorable relationships" with those whom CPCUs serve, and are contrary to the "public interest" concept that constitutes the goal of the entire Code. While the Canons and Guidelines are not themselves enforceable, the BEI may use them to interpret the Rules and apply them to specific factual situations. Here, for instance, they clarify the intended meaning of R3.1 and support the BEI's conclusion that it was violated.

White's conduct is not excused by either alleged or actual ignorance of the Code because R1.1 clearly gives him "a duty to understand and abide by all the Rules," regardless of whether they are violated in practice by others who are not subject to the Code. Nor can White's conduct be excused because he delegated the actual claim handling to the adjuster. White violated R1.2 by advocating, sanctioning, participating in, causing to be accomplished, carrying out through another, or condoning an act that he is prohibited from performing under the Rules. The adjuster's conduct is likewise in violation of Rules R3.1, R3.3, and R6.1. R1.2 clarifies that such violations are not excused merely because the violator allegedly or actually followed superiors' instructions.

Although the BEI believes that both White and the adjuster engaged in unethical conduct, it would consider additional evidence before determining disciplinary actions. At a minimum, the BEI would send each violator a letter notifying the violators that the BEI had ruled the conduct to be unethical. It would request each violator to cease and desist from engaging in such conduct, and it would warn each of the potential consequences of continuing Rule violations. If a violator failed to cease and desist or was later found guilty of additional violations, or if the original investigation and hearing process disclosed adverse evidence not originally apparent, the BEI would probably impose or recommend stronger sanctions. The adjuster, a candidate, could have his CPCU designation withheld until he provided convincing proof of rehabilitation. White could be subject to reprimand, censure, or revocation or suspension of his CPCU designation.

The claimant, as a party directly involved, would be notified of the decision and the penalties imposed. She would also be told that the BEI cannot intervene on her behalf in any legal dispute with the insurer. The BEI may disclose the decisions and penalties to officers and chapters of the CPCU Society, as well as to the parties directly involved. Any publication of sanctions to others, as in a public censure, must first be approved by the Ethics Policy Committee of the Board of Trustees.

CASE HCS-103—Fraudulent Conduct

Keisha Abbot, CPCU, and Carl Alverez, CPCU, own and operate a combination real estate and general insurance agency. Abbot manages most of the insurance activities, while Alverez concentrates on the real estate portion of the business. Alverez bought 500 acres of swampland for $5 an acre, ran full-page ads in various publications promoting its sale, eventually sold the land at an average of $4,000 for each half-acre plot, and split the proceeds with Abbot in accordance with the partnership agreement.

A couple who purchased one of the plots provides the Ethics Counsel with evidence that they bought the land only because the advertisement said the subdivision already had paved streets and sidewalks, city water, two swimming pools, tennis courts, a clubhouse, and free lifetime healthcare for the first twenty couples to buy at least one plot. None of these improvements and benefits was available when the couple arrived at the swamp. Abbot contends that she personally did not violate the Code because the insurance aspects of the business were conducted legally and ethically. Alverez contends that his real estate activities are not related to insurance, and hence, his status as a CPCU.

OPINION HCS-103—Fraudulent Conduct

The standards most directly applicable to this case are those contained in Rules R1.1, R1.2, R3.1, R3.2, R3.3, and R6.1; Guidelines G1.2, G1.3, G3.3, and G3.4; and Canons 1, 3, and 6. Though not specifically mentioned in the information given, the BEI assumes that both Abbot and Alverez were bound by the Rules, either by voluntary election or by virtue of their CPCU conferment dates.

The BEI believes the conduct of Abbot and Alverez was unethical. First, the evidence indicates that they violated one or more laws (a breach of R3.3) and that they should have kept informed on such laws (in accord with R6.1 and G3.4). Furthermore, Alverez's real estate scheme constituted "an act or omission of a dishonest, deceitful, or fraudulent nature" (thus violating the letter of R3.1 and the spirit of Canons 1, 3, and 6); the scheme raises serious questions about possible violations of R3.2 (as clarified in G3.3); and Abbot and Alverez have a duty to "understand and abide by all Rules of conduct" as specified in R1.1. The BEI must determine whether Alverez's real estate scheme is outside the purview of the Code, as he contends, and whether Abbot's lack of direct involvement excuses her conduct.

Alverez's real estate scheme is definitely within the purview of the Code and the jurisdiction of the BEI. He is a CPCU and bound by the Rules. R3.1 clearly prohibits him from engaging in acts or omissions of a dishonest, deceitful, or fraudulent nature "in the conduct of business or professional activities." Alverez is also subject to disciplinary action, under R3.3, for the violation of "any law or regulation."

The BEI would recommend that Alverez's CPCU designation be suspended indefinitely or revoked. The final decision would be made by the Ethics Policy Committee of the Board of Trustees. Abbot's lack of direct involvement in the real estate scheme does not excuse the fact that she, too, was guilty of Rule violations. R1.2 stipulates the following:

> A CPCU shall not advocate, sanction, participate in, cause to be accomplished, otherwise carry out through another, or condone any act the CPCU is prohibited from performing by the Rules of the Code.

Even if Abbot could prove that she did not advocate or participate in the scheme, the BEI may presume that she condoned it by failing to object and by accepting her share of the proceeds. If Abbot did not inquire about the source of her nearly $2 million gain, she would probably be guilty of complicity under the law, and she would also be in violation of R3.2 (allowing the pursuit of financial gain to interfere with the exercise of sound professional judgment) and R4.1 (failing to discharge occupational duties competently). Accordingly, the BEI would recommend to the Ethics Policy Committee that Abbot's CPCU designation be suspended indefinitely or revoked.

If the Ethics Policy Committee agreed with these recommendations, the decisions would be published widely and conveyed to the complainants. If their designations were suspended, Abbot and Alverez would be given an opportunity to offer proof of rehabilitation.

CASE HCS-104—Complaint Requirements and Commissions

David Crowley, CPCU, is the brother of a county politician who arranged for him to be broker-of-record on all insurance policies purchased by the county. Though the gross commission Crowley receives on this insurance is about $100,000 per year, virtually all of the everyday service work is performed by county and insurance company employees. Crowley's role is to place the coverage with the insurers on any cancellation or renewal dates, the coverage having been secured initially by a previous agent. Shortly before the renewal date of one of the policies, Crowley obtained premium quotations from two insurers, A and B. Company B quoted a lower price and offered better coverage than Company A, but Crowley selected Company A because it paid him a substantially higher commission rate (on a larger total premium).

Although never explicitly requested to do so, Crowley contributed generously to his brother's political party, frequently entertained county employees on his yacht, and gave his brother the down payment for a new home.

Crowley's principal competitor, also a CPCU and a broker, reports this information in a telephone conversation with the Ethics Counsel, but indicates that he does not want his name revealed or to testify in any disciplinary proceedings. He also says that one of the county's insurers selected by Crowley was rumored to be in financial trouble. Suppose a taxpayer brought the charges of ethical impropriety to the American Institute.

OPINION HCS-104—Complaint Requirements and Commissions

In this case, the first issue the BEI considers is the competitor's refusal to testify or allow his name to be used. Because one of the constitutional requirements of due process is the right of an accused to be confronted by his or her accuser(s), the American Institute's Disciplinary Rules and Procedures (sections IV. A., B.) provide that all complaints alleging a violation of the Code be submitted in writing to Counsel and signed by the complainant. If the competitor refused to submit a complaint in writing and sign it, and if no other party were willing to do so, the complaint would be dismissed. Any person may file a complaint against a CPCU or a CPCU candidate, as long as the complaint complies with the Disciplinary Rules and Procedures. However, if Crowley received his CPCU designation before July 1976 and he had not filed a voluntary written election to be bound by the Rules, the case would be dismissed for lack of jurisdiction.

While the competitor's attitude is contrary to the goal of Canon 9, no basis exists for a disciplinary action against him because he did not explicitly violate a Rule. R9.2 does not obligate the competitor to sign a complaint or testify. It only obligates him to reveal, upon request, any information he may have concerning an alleged violation of the Code, nor is he obligated to volunteer any information, except in the situation covered by R9.3 (and clarified in G9.2).

Assuming that the initial investigation eventually resulted in a proper complaint and sufficient evidence of possible misconduct to justify a formal hearing, the standards most directly applicable to Crowley would be Rules R2.1, R3.1, R3.2, R3.3, and R6.1; Guidelines G1.2, G3.1, G3.3, and G3.4; and Canons 1 and 3.

The political contributions, entertainment, and/or down payment on his brother's home could meet the applicable tests for rebating commissions illegally, in which case Crowley violated R3.3 and would be subject to discipline. Though the BEI will not act solely on the basis of a rumor, if the evidence showed that Crowley had recommended an insurer he knew to be in financial trouble, he clearly violated R3.1 (a "dishonest, deceitful, or fraudulent" act, as clarified in G3.1).

If he did not know of the insurer's financial difficulties, the BEI may investigate whether Crowley had complied with his minimum continuing education obligation under R2.1.

Crowley's acceptance of commissions for work performed largely by others, though legal on its face, also raises the question of whether he violated R3.2 or G1.2 and G3.3. The BEI acknowledges that the acceptance of such compensation, which is not for and commensurate with services actually rendered or to be rendered, is contrary to the goals of G1.2 and G3.3, but finds no evidence that such acceptance violated R3.2. However, the BEI feels that Crowley probably did violate R3.2, as well as R3.1, by placing some of the insurance with the insurer who offered higher commissions and lesser coverage. This conclusion is supported by G3.3, though it obviously assumes that placing the insurance with the other insurer would have better met the consumer's legitimate needs and best interests, the actual determination of which would require additional information.

While the investigation and hearings process may prove otherwise, Crowley may have violated as many as six Rules of professional conduct. If he were found guilty on all counts, the BEI would recommend suspension of his CPCU designation. If he were found guilty on at least one but not all the counts, a lesser penalty might be imposed, especially if he had not violated any law.

CASE HCS-105—Business Decisions and Ethical Conduct

John Keller, CPCU, chief executive officer of a capital stock insurer, canceled the agency contracts of all the company's agents in a particular state because of the poor loss ratio on auto insurance business. As a result, thousands of motorists had difficulty securing replacement coverage, and many ended up in the state's assigned risk plan. "My first and most important responsibility is to our stockholders," Keller says when asked about the ethical propriety of his decision. "The rates in that state are not adequate to make a profit."

OPINION HCS-105—Business Decisions and Ethical Conduct

The standards most directly applicable to this case are those in Rules R1.1, R3.1, R3.3, R4.1, and R4.2; Guidelines G1.1, G1.2, G1.3, and G4.2; and Canons 1, 3, 4, and 6.

The BEI assumes that a proper complaint has been filed, that Keller is bound by the Rules, and that the complaint has alleged violations of these specific Rules. Though the complainant need not be a person directly harmed by the conduct in question, it is reasonable to assume that this complaint probably would have been brought by a former agent and/or former policyholder. It is likewise reasonable to assume that Keller's decision did not violate any law or regulation. If so, the BEI would not further consider R3.3, and the inquiry would focus on whether any other ethics Rule had been violated.

The BEI is not empowered to take disciplinary action unless a Rule has been violated. Thus, because the BEI finds no evidence of any Rule violation, it would dismiss this case on its merits.

The BEI disagrees with Keller's contention that his first and most important responsibility is to his stockholders. While Keller's occupational duties make him directly answerable to his board of directors and ultimately to the shareholders, his first and most important responsibility as a CPCU is his ethical responsibility to understand and abide by the Rules of professional conduct. Though his occupational duties would seldom, if ever, conflict with the Rules, his status as a CPCU makes him answerable to the Code should a conflict arise. He could, for example, maximize short-run returns through conduct that is legal but prohibited under the Code. In such a case, he would be subject to disciplinary action on ethics grounds.

What excused Keller's conduct was not that he has responsibility to shareholders, but that he did not violate any Rules. His decision to cancel the agency contracts was not "dishonest, deceitful, or fraudulent" (R3.1), and no evidence indicates that he failed to support the kinds of improvements called for in R4.2 and G4.2. Some may argue that his decision was contrary to the goals of Canon 1 (serving the public interest) and Canon 3 (avoiding unjust harm to others).

It could also be argued that he failed to maintain dignified and honorable relationships with agents and policyholders (in accord with the spirit of Canon 6). Yet it could just as well be argued that the spirit of these three Canons would have been more seriously breached if the company had continued to do business in that state at the permitted rate levels and then become financially insolvent. Such arguments are not sufficient to support an ethics disciplinary action in the absence of a Rule violation.

CASE HCS-106—Ethics and Advertising

Polly Browne, CPCU, is director of advertising and public relations for a large insurer that specializes in individual health insurance. Browne approved copy for various media advertisements that said "we will write health insurance for you even if you are sick or disabled or have been turned down by other insurers.... In fact, we will write health insurance for anyone, regardless of age or health." A competitor insurer accuses Browne of Code violations because the ad did not specify that the insurance always contains a very restrictive exclusion for preexisting conditions.

OPINION HCS-106—Ethics and Advertising

This case could involve violations of laws or regulations governing deceptive advertising and, thus, the application of R3.3. However, the Opinion focuses on the standards contained in Rules R3.1 and R7.2, Guidelines G3.1 and G7.4, and Canons 3 and 7. The BEI assumes that Browne did not intend to defraud anyone. It must therefore determine whether her approval of the advertising copy constituted an omission of a dishonest or deceitful nature (under R3.1) and/or a misrepresentation of the "limitations of...any product...of an insurer" (under R7.2).

Though G3.1 permits Browne to determine how much information the advertisement should volunteer, it also prevents her from concealing facts that are material to determining the limitations of an insurance contract. G7.4 explicitly instructs her not to engage in deceptive advertising practices that significantly mislead the public. The BEI believes Browne violated both of the applicable Rules. Advertising copy cannot list all of the exclusions and limitations of an insurance contract. In this case, the public would be misled by the failure to at least mention the preexisting conditions exclusion because the copy itself suggests otherwise.

The BEI would probably issue an informal admonition requesting Browne alter the advertising copy to conform to the letter and spirit of the Code. Stronger sanctions would be imposed only if she failed to comply. The BEI believes that comparatively mild disciplinary action is appropriate in this case because of the inherent difficulties posed by the nature of advertising. Unless she blatantly disregards the BEI's initial admonitions, it seems enough to remind her that her Code obligations require more than advertising be truthful.

CASE HCS-107—Consultant Recommendations

Luke Mansur, CPCU, operates his own small insurance consulting business solely in a state that does not require him to be licensed either as a consultant or as an agent or a broker. Mansur has extensive business insurance experience and is highly regarded by the corporate clients for whom he consults. He charges all consulting clients a fee of $150 per hour (plus expenses) for his services, which consist largely of devising bid specifications for various kinds of insurance, soliciting competitive bids, analyzing the bid proposals, and making recommendations to the client-buyer. Mansur does not recommend agents or brokers per se. Instead, he allows the buyer to decide whether he is to solicit bids from agents and brokers specified by the buyer or advertise openly for bids from any interested party. Mansur recommends that one large corporate client discontinue a particular insurance policy at its renewal date, replace it with aggregate and specific excess-of-loss coverage with large deductibles, and handle the underlying loss exposure with a carefully planned program of funded retention. He also recommends that the client study the feasibility of forming or acquiring its own captive insurer.

A local agent alleges that Mansur is guilty of highly unethical conduct because he always recommends self-insurance, his fees are too high, and he is not a licensed agent or a member of the agents' association. Another agent objects to what he calls the unfair competition of Mansur allowing only selected agents to bid for the better clients-buyers. A third agent challenges the ethics of competitive bidding for private corporations and always recommending to them the lowest-priced bid.

OPINION HCS-107—Consultant Recommendations

The standards that may apply most directly to this case are those contained in Rules R3.2, R4.1, R7.1, and R7.2; Guidelines G3.3 and G7.5; and Canons 3, 4, and 7. However, because no evidence exists that Mansur violated any Rules, the case would be dismissed on its merits.

Despite the three local agents' allegations, the law does not require Mansur to be licensed or to join the agents' association, and nothing in his conduct, bidding procedures, or recommendations violates laws, regulations, or other standards in the ethics Code. Mansur appears to be competently and consistently discharging his duties in full compliance with R4.1. Recommendations concerning deductibles, funded retention, and the feasibility of captive insurers may even be ethically required in situations where they best serve the client's interests, by the dictates of R7.1, R7.2, and G7.5. Such recommendations are not by themselves unethical in the present case. If Mansur always recommended self-insurance and/or the lowest-priced bid, as was alleged, it would raise questions about both his competence and his ethics. But no evidence supports these allegations.

The BEI assumes that the client-buyer agreed in advance to pay Mansur $150 per hour for agreed-upon services and that he actually delivered those services. Therefore, the fee was neither "at the expense of the uninformed" nor "unconscionable" within the meaning of G3.3, nor did it violate R3.2, because the evidence suggests that Mansur's recommendations were in his clients' best interests. He did not allow the pursuit of financial gain to interfere with the exercise of his sound professional judgment and skills.

The BEI would not apply R3.2 to judge the level of compensation a CPCU receives in the marketplace for his or her services because the absolute level of compensation does not make professional services ethically suspect. If the pursuit of any amount of financial gain caused Mansur to make judgments that were not in the best interests of those served, then those services would be suspect.

CASE HCS-108—Use of CPCU Letters

After earning his CPCU designation, insurance agent Jason Fleming joined his local CPCU Society chapter. During an e-mail exchange, another chapter member noticed that Jason's e-mail address was jflemingcpcu@abc.net. The member mentioned to Jason that he thought such use of the CPCU designation was prohibited by the Code. One of Jason's competitors noted his e-mail address and discovered that Jason's Web site was www.cpcuagent.com. The competitor, also a CPCU, registers a complaint with the Ethics Counsel about Jason's use of the CPCU letters in his e-mail and Web site addresses.

OPINION HCS-108—Use of CPCU Letters

The standards most directly applicable to this case are those in Rules R1.1, R3.3, and R8.1; Guidelines G8.1.a.3 and G8.1.e; and Canons 1, 3, and 8.

Jason's e-mail and Web site addresses violate Rule R8.1 by failing to adhere to Guideline G8.1.a.3's prescribed use of the CPCU letters. G8.1a.3 states that the initials CPCU should not be used as part of a logo, or be affixed to any object, product, or property, for any purpose whatsoever, except by the American Institute.

Because he failed to contact the BEI to apply for approval to use the initials CPCU in his e-mail address and Web site, he is also in violation of Guideline G8.1e. Even if he had sought it, Jason would not have received permission to use the initials for advertising purposes.

The BEI would order Jason Fleming to cease and desist using his e-mail and Web site addresses. Were he to continue his unauthorized use of the CPCU letters, legal action and disciplinary penalties would follow.

CASE HCS-109—Misrepresentation

Carl Chen, CPCU, a field representative of a small multiline insurer, is making a sales presentation with an agent who is not a CPCU. Acquiring the account would greatly enhance Chen's position with the company because it is a prestigious account and a sales campaign is in progress. Part of the proposal is a business package policy with a $1,000 deductible applicable to the property coverages.

In his zeal to make the sale, Chen fails to disclose the deductible. He feels no guilt because he knows that many of his competitors do not mention deductibles unless specifically asked by the applicant or insured. If a complaint is received from the insured, should any disciplinary action be taken against Chen?

OPINION HCS-109—Misrepresentation

The standards most directly applicable to this are those in Rules R3.1 and R7.2, Guidelines G3.1, and Canons 3 and 7.

Because it does not appear that Chen was guilty of a misrepresentation within the meaning of R7.2, the BEI must determine whether his failure to disclose a policy provision constituted a violation of R3.1 and, specifically, whether his nondisclosure was an "omission of a dishonest, deceitful, or fraudulent nature."

Guideline G3.1 illustrates the general kinds of acts and omissions that can violate R3.1 and that normally "would cause unjust harm to others," thereby violating the spirit of Canon 3. The Guideline explicitly stipulates, "A CPCU should neither misrepresent nor conceal a fact or information that is material to determining the…scope or limitations of an insurance contract." However, the Guideline also states that "…the extent to which a CPCU should volunteer information and facts must necessarily be left to sound professional judgment." It seems clear, therefore, that an omission would violate R3.1 if, based on sound professional judgment, the voluntary disclosure of facts or information is required by the circumstances because the disclosure is material to the buyer's decision making and necessary to avoid what would otherwise cause unjust harm to others.

This type of nondisclosure may be common among his competitors, as Chen contends, but his ethical obligations are prescribed by the Code. The BEI believes that Chen violated R3.1, that he was aware of his ethical obligations under the Rule, and that he felt himself to be excused by the practices of others (many of whom are not subject to the Code). The BEI would at least issue a private admonition requesting Chen cease and desist. The disciplinary penalty may be more severe if sufficient evidence of fraud exists and/or if the insured had been significantly harmed. Regardless, the insured would be reminded that the BEI's action under the Code is independent of any legal remedies the insured may have.

CASE HCS-110—Ethics Violations for Discrimination

Helen Gray, CPCU, is an auto underwriter with the Fire and Casualty Company. Her job includes the selection and rejection of applicants for auto insurance and requires that she determine the class into which an applicant is placed. All applicants are categorized as either "above average" or "below average." The premium charged is considerably higher for below-average insureds.

One of the agents in her territory is Lynn Finch, who also runs a foreign car agency. Finch's business is dominated by residents of an economically disadvantaged section of the city, most of whom share a particular ethnicity. Gray has automatically classed these applicants as below average because she believes that they are bad risks. No available data, however, indicate a higher-than-average loss ratio in that geographical area. Has Gray violated the ethics Code?

OPINION HCS-110—Ethics Violations for Discrimination

In most jurisdictions, underwriting practices predicated on the ethnic origin of the applicant (or insured) would constitute unlawful discrimination under applicable state and federal statutes and regulations. Therefore, Gray's practice would likewise be a violation of R3.3 under the Code, and she would be subject to disciplinary action. If she attempted to plead ignorance of the applicable law, she would be acknowledging that she also violated R2.1 and R6.1. An underwriter who is not familiar with antidiscrimination laws is violating her duty to "keep informed on those technical matters that are essential to the maintenance of [her] professional competence," as well as her duty to "keep informed on the legal limitations imposed upon the scope of…professional duties."

Assuming Gray did violate one or more Rules, she would at least be issued an informal admonition to cease and desist. Additionally, she would be warned that any additional Rule violation would subject her to the possibility of more severe penalties.

If Gray did not in fact violate any law or regulation, the case would be dismissed on its merits. A CPCU is not guilty of an ethics violation for discrimination unless it is unlawful discrimination (and therefore a breach of R3.3) or the discrimination itself is lawful but otherwise involves an act or omission prohibited by the Rules.

CASE HCS-111— Occupational Safety and Health Act Violations

A CPCU who is a loss prevention engineer employed by an insurance company believes that an insured firm is engaging in practices that violate many of the requirements of the Occupational Safety and Health Act. The CPCU reports these violations to the insurer's underwriting department but not to the Occupational Safety and Health Administration (OSHA).

To what extent, if any, is the CPCU subject to discipline under the Code?

OPINION HCS-111— Occupational Safety and Health Act Violations

Under certain circumstances, this case may involve violations of laws or regulations (and therefore, the application of R3.3 as well as related Rules and Guidelines). However, the Opinion focuses on the standards contained in Rules R4.1, R5.4, R6.2, and R7.2; Guidelines G4.7, G6.6, and G7.2; and Canons 6 and 7.

The Opinion assumes that a proper complaint has been brought and that the engineer is subject to the binding effect of the Rules. It also assumes that the engineer informed the insured firm of the practices he believed were not in compliance with OSHA, in which case he did not violate R7.2 or the spirit of G7.2 and Canon 7. Had he represented that the firm was in full compliance with OSHA, he would have violated R3.1 (by committing, in the conduct of his professional activities, an act of a dishonest nature). In fact, even if the firm appeared to be in full compliance with OSHA, he should clarify to the insured firm that his belief is merely a professional opinion; otherwise, he would run the danger of violating R7.2 ("A CPCU shall not misrepresent the…limitations or any…service of an insurer").

By disclosing this information to his underwriting department, the engineer did not violate R6.2 because such disclosure is specifically permitted when "made to a person who necessarily must have the information in order to discharge occupational or professional duties." The engineer's disclosure to underwriting is consistent with his R4.1 duty to "competently…discharge [his own] occupational duties." Furthermore, his failure to report the firm's practices to OSHA does not violate R5.4. The latter Rule does not obligate him to volunteer information. It only obligates him to disclose information officially requested by appropriate regulatory authorities, and then only regarding laws governing the qualifications or conduct of insurance practitioners. The case, therefore, would be dismissed on its merits.

CASE HCS-112—Occupational Duties

A CPCU who is a full-time risk manager regularly renews his employer's insurance with the same insurers year after year, refusing insurance agents' requests for specifications to be used for competitive bids. The CPCU's refusal is based on an honest, but a mistaken, belief that the insurance that the company currently carries provides the best available coverage and claim service at the lowest available cost. No complaint has been filed with the BEI.

Is this CPCU subject to discipline for violation of the Code? May the agent, who is a CPCU candidate, call the matter to the BEI's attention? If so, what are the required procedures?

OPINION HCS-112—Occupational Duties

To clarify the procedural question, suppose that a member of the BEI read in the newspaper about a person who had been indicted for embezzlement and that the member knew that the indicted person was a CPCU. This would prompt an investigation at the BEI's initiative. However, the BEI is usually not aware of an alleged Code violation until someone voluntarily reports it to the Ethics Counsel. Anyone may report an alleged violation or file a formal complaint as long as the complaint is in compliance with the American Institute's published Disciplinary Rules and Procedures.

In this case, suppose that the agent reported an alleged Rule violation. Unless the agent signed a written complaint or his informal oral report prompted an investigation that later revealed sufficient evidence of a possible Rule violation, the case would be dismissed as without merit. Therefore, assume that the risk manager has been appropriately accused of violating Rule R4.1 and the spirit of Canon 4.

Rule R4.1 stipulates, "A CPCU shall competently and consistently discharge his or her occupational duties." Nonetheless, Guideline G4.1 clarifies the following:

> …[the BEI] will not intervene or arbitrate between the parties in an employment, or a contractual, relationship….Nor are the American Institute's disciplinary procedures a substitute for legal and other remedies available to such parties. In the event of an alleged violation of Rule R4.1, therefore, the Board will hear the case only after all other remedies have been exhausted….

As an employee, the risk manager has an employment relationship with his employer-firm. His employer is the primary party to whom his occupational duties are owed. If the risk manager is guilty of failing to discharge his occupational duties competently and consistently, the employer may dismiss him and/or take other appropriate actions. If no such actions are taken by the employer or other affected parties (for example, the stockholders), the BEI will not hear the case.

G4.1 further states that, even when all other remedies have been exhausted, the BEI will take disciplinary action under the following circumstances:

> ...a proven violation has caused unjust harm to another person, and the violation brings substantial discredit upon the CPCU designation; or it would otherwise be in the public interest to take disciplinary action under the Code.

Because no evidence exists that either of these two criteria are met in this case, the BEI would not take disciplinary action under R4.1.

By renewing his firm's insurance with the same insurers yearly, the risk manager may be acting competently. The facts also may reveal a human error in judgment that would not violate the Rule. Even if the facts support a finding of incompetence on the risk manager's part, the other (G4.1) prerequisites of disciplinary action are not met in this case. The only basis of disciplinary action is that he may have violated R2.1 (that is, he may have failed to keep informed on those matters essential to the maintenance of his professional competence as a risk manager). As indicated in G2.3, "if a CPCU is accused of violating any other Rule, the Board may, at its discretion, require the accused to furnish evidence of compliance with Rule R2.1." Such evidence of compliance is especially likely to be sought in cases involving allegations of incompetence.

Finally, the rationale of G4.1 is not limited to cases involving the employer-employee relationship. It applies to any alleged violation of R4.1, that is, to any case in which a CPCU (or CPCU candidate) is accused of failing to discharge his or her occupational duties competently and consistently. The BEI will not hear the case unless all other available remedies have been exhausted.

CASE HCS-113—Disclosure of Material Facts

A CPCU who is an agent is negotiating manuscript products liability coverage with an insurance company underwriter. He doubts that the underwriter is aware that the Consumer Product Safety Commission (CPSC) is considering investigating the safety of one of his client's products. An unfavorable finding by the CPSC is likely to force the client-company to incur large product recall expenses, which will be covered by the policy being negotiated if it is issued. The agent does not mention to the underwriter this possible action, and the underwriter does not ask about any such action. To what extent, if any, is this CPCU subject to discipline under the Code? If the CPCU were a broker instead of an agent, would this be material to the BEI's findings?

OPINION HCS-113—Disclosure of Material Facts

Although the agent has a contractual relationship with his insurer-principal, the BEI assumes he was not accused of violating R4.1. Therefore, it may hear the case, apart from any remedies available to the insurer.

The BEI must determine whether the agent violated his R3.1 duty by engaging in an "act or omission of a dishonest, deceitful, or fraudulent nature." Generally speaking, because underwriting techniques and requirements vary considerably among insurers, the BEI believes it would be unreasonable to expect an agent to know every kind of information a particular underwriter would deem material to the writing of a particular kind of insurance. Therefore, the BEI sees no ethical reason for an agent to volunteer information in his or her possession except when the information is specifically requested in the application; the information is specifically requested by the underwriter or other authorized employee of the insurer; or the agent knows that the information is material to most insurers writing the kind of insurance in question, and the agent has good reason to believe the insurer cannot readily discover the information through inspection or other commonly used sources of underwriting information. (That he or she should know these things is reinforced by R2.1.) As indicated in G3.1, "The extent to which a CPCU should volunteer information and facts must necessarily be left to sound professional judgment." These criteria are provided to assist agent-CPCUs in making sound professional judgments about the disclosure of information to underwriters.

In this case, the agent should at least have known that the information could affect the insurer's underwriting decision or the pricing of the insurance. He, therefore, was guilty of concealing a material fact, ethically if not legally.

He violated R3.1 by engaging in an omission of a dishonest or deceitful nature (whether the omission was also fraudulent would depend on his intent). He also may have violated R3.2 by allowing "the pursuit of financial gain...to interfere with the exercise of sound professional judgment and skills." The BEI would reprimand the agent in the form of an informal rebuke with limited publication. If satisfactory evidence of fraud existed, the BEI would recommend public censure or suspension of the CPCU designation, and the final decision would be made by the Ethics Policy Committee of the American Institute's Board of Trustees.

The BEI would reach the same conclusion if the accused had been a broker instead of an agent. Although the legal duties of the two may differ somewhat, both have ethical duties to their clients, and both are summoned by Canon 1 to put the public interest above their own.

CASE HCS-114—Violation of Law or Regulation

A CPCU who is a risk manager has purchased for his firm, in the nonadmitted market, insurance coverage the risk manager knows is available in the admitted market, but at a higher premium than the nonadmitted coverage. The CPCU knows that the broker through whom the nonadmitted coverage was purchased did not comply with the applicable surplus lines law. Has the risk manager violated any Rules under the Code?

OPINION HCS-114—Violation of Law or Regulation

Though most surplus lines laws contain several specific exemptions that may excuse the conduct of the broker and the risk manager, the BEI assumes that the broker violated the applicable law. The BEI has no jurisdiction over the broker because he is not a CPCU or CPCU candidate. It must therefore determine whether the CPCU risk manager has violated any Rules.

Though the risk manager did not violate a law or regulation (and therefore is not subject to discipline under R3.3), he did violate his R1.2 duty. He may not have advocated or sanctioned the broker's conduct, but did "otherwise carry out through another or condone" an act (violating the law) that he himself is prohibited from performing by the Rules. The risk manager would be informally admonished for unethical conduct and given a reasonable length of time to make satisfactory insurance arrangements for his firm. In some states, for example, he may be able to obtain the commissioner's approval of an arrangement that would, in the absence of such approval, violate the surplus lines law. If he could not do so, he would be ethically obligated to place the insurance with an authorized insurer, even if it meant higher premiums for his employer firm.

The risk manager would not be obligated by R5.4 to report the broker's law violation unless the risk manager had been properly subpoenaed by the appropriate regulatory authorities in the process of investigating or prosecuting the broker's alleged violation of the insurance laws. In fact, this case may never be brought to the BEI's attention. It is conceivable that a commissioner or an authorized insurer would register an ethics complaint. But the broker or employer-policyholder would not.

Suppose a case with essentially the same facts involved two CPCUs who are brokers in competition for the risk manager's account, and assume that one broker had secured the account with a lower premium proposal from an unauthorized insurer, in violation of the surplus lines law. Realistically, a competitor broker, having been harmed, is more likely to file an ethics complaint with the BEI.

CASE HCS-115—Dishonest Acts in Business and Profession

Eric Patel, CPA, CPCU, is the treasurer of a large insurance company. To induce Stan Brown, a potential investor, to purchase a substantial portion of the company's new bond issue, Patel intentionally certified the financial status of XYZ Corporation, the manufacturer of firefighting equipment, as sound. In fact, Patel knew the XYZ Corporation was nearly insolvent, but he was persuaded to do so by his brother-in-law, the president of XYZ Corporation, in the honest belief that without the successful sale of the bond issue several hundred employees of XYZ would lose their jobs.

After Brown had purchased the bonds, the scheme was discovered, and Patel, in addition to criminal penalties, was disciplined by the State Institute of Certified Public Accountants.

Is Patel subject to disciplinary action under the Code if it can be shown by proper evidence that:

(a) He personally and financially benefited from his illegal act?

or

(b) He was solely motivated by his concern for the jobs involved, and no one sustained any loss in consequence of his act?

or

(c) XYZ Corporation was not a manufacturer, but a large insurance brokerage firm; otherwise, the facts are the same as in (b)?

OPINION HCS-115—Dishonest Acts in Business and Profession

Patel violated his R3.1 duty by engaging in an "act or omission of a dishonest, deceitful, or fraudulent nature." Because this Rule applies to any "business or professional activities," whether XYZ Corporation was an insurance brokerage firm or a manufacturer, as asked in hypothetical question (c), is irrelevant.

Patel also violated the security laws. He is therefore subject to disciplinary action under R3.3, as further clarified under G3.4. If Patel financially benefited from his act, as suggested in hypothetical question (a), he also violated R3.2 by allowing the pursuit of financial gain to interfere with the exercise of sound professional judgments and skills. In view of the criminal conviction, the BEI would immediately suspend his CPCU designation. If the Ethics Policy Committee concurred with the recommendation, the suspension would remain in effect until Patel could provide proof of rehabilitation.

Hypothetical question (b) changes the circumstances by assuming that Patel was motivated solely by an altruistic concern for the employees and that no one sustained any loss as a consequence of his act. His motivations do not alter the conclusion that he violated the Code. When criminal conviction is not involved, a violator's motivations may be taken into consideration, along with other factors, in determining the severity of the penalty to be imposed.

CASE HCS-116—Dignified and Honorable Relationships With Competitors

A CPCU reviews an insurance portfolio with a prospective new client (a gas station operator) and finds a garage liability policy that expired forty-five days previously. The policy includes a thirty-day binder and a cover letter from the present agent stating that the renewal policy would be mailed within ten days. Nothing has been received in the interim. The new agent says the following:

> The facts are that you have no proof of coverage at all, and if you were sued because of an injury here or arising out of the operation of your car or wrecker, you might find yourself high and dry. You may be able to eventually recover the damages from the insurance company or the agent, but it might be very difficult for you to do it—and it might cost you a lot in terms of time and legal expense. It appears that your agent has mishandled your account, and I recommend that you get new coverage into effect immediately. I can leave a written binder with you right now and will have the new policy back here within ten days.

The gas station operator agrees. The former agent learns of this discussion two weeks later when he delivers the "renewal policy." He contends that the CPCU's action was unethical and that the situation demanded a telephone call to find out whether a current binder was in effect. He files a formal complaint.

OPINION HCS-116—Dignified and Honorable Relationships With Competitors

The CPCU's conduct may have been contrary to the spirit of Canon 6 and Guidelines G6.1 and G6.2, which direct a CPCU to strive for dignified and honorable relationships with competitors. Against this it can be argued that his conduct did not cause "unjust harm to others" within the meaning of Canon 3. Vigorous competition is often in the public interest, and it is not inherently unethical to offer improvements in a prospective client's insurance arrangements. An agent who did not do so ordinarily would be violating the R4.1 obligation to discharge his or her occupational duties competently.

Yet, whenever an insurance advisor convinces a client of the need to effect improvements in existing insurance arrangements, the client may infer that his or her previous advisors were careless or incompetent. The BEI sees no ethical reason why an agent should be required to share with a competitor a lawful and desirable trade advantage. The BEI is not empowered to take disciplinary action unless the Code has been violated.

The only Rule potentially applicable to this case is R3.2, which imposes a duty to refrain from allowing the pursuit of financial gain to interfere with the exercise of sound professional judgment, and it should be interpreted within the context of Canon 3. The CPCU's use of phrases like "mishandled your account" borders on the indiscreet. But the BEI finds no evidence of unsound professional judgment that would cause unjust harm to others. Accordingly, the case would be dismissed on its merits.

CASE HCS-117—CPCU Examination Preparation

A CPCU who is a part-time university professor planned to offer a Saturday morning CPCU 510 class from 8:00 AM to noon on the first Saturday of the month. The local CPCU chapter expressed concern about his ability to present all material through lectures and handout materials without requiring students to study the textbook, and believed that the professor's class would conflict with its plans to hold a similar class on Tuesday evenings.

The professor dismissed the first point by noting that he had previously run a successful Naval Reserve Class on exactly the same basis. He also believed that participants in his class would be unlikely to register for the Tuesday night class.

An American Institute staff member called the professor to discuss the potential educational pitfalls in the lecture-and-handout approach. The professor indicated that because he already had thirty students who had submitted their $300, he felt obligated to proceed with the plan.

At the end of the year, the roster-sheet report to the professor revealed a course effectiveness ratio that was approximately one-third that of the national average. Concurrent with the receipt of the roster-sheet feedback, the chapter president noted that the professor was planning another CPCU 510 class offering on the same basis. When asked about this, the professor replied, "While there had been some problems with the group, I don't see any justification for concluding that the format was the problem."

The second year proceeded exactly the same as the first and yielded almost identical results. The chapter president contacted the professor in mid-June and discovered that the professor was going to reoffer this course. The chapter president asks for American Institute assistance through involvement of the BEI.

OPINION HCS-117—CPCU Examination Preparation

The American Institute does not require any particular method of preparing for CPCU examinations. Nor would an instructor who taught a course such as the professor's violate any law. Therefore, the issue in this case is whether the professor's approach is otherwise unethical under the Code.

Unless a formal complaint was filed against the professor, the case would be dismissed. Even a complaint would likewise be dismissed unless satisfactory evidence of a Rule violation existed. If a complaint was filed in this case, it would probably allege violations of R6.3, R4.1, and R3.2.

Rule 6.3 stipulates that a "CPCU shall not knowingly misrepresent or conceal any limitations on his or her ability to provide the…quality of professional services the circumstances require." The professor could have violated the Rule by misrepresenting the quality of his services, especially if he led students to believe he would guarantee that they would pass the examination. But no evidence of this exists.

The criteria of G4.1 may allow the BEI to hear an allegation of incompetence under R4.1. Nonetheless, the application of the Rule is complicated because most CPCU instructors are part-time volunteers whose primary occupational duties are owed to employers or clients. Additionally, evaluating an instructor's competence is an inherently difficult task because CPCU instructors are not employed by the American Institute, professional educators do not agree on all of the criteria and methods that should be used to evaluate teaching competence, and many variables affect the results of a learning opportunity.

Consequently, the BEI cannot find, in R4.1, any basis for disciplining an instructor on ethics grounds. (An instructor could of course be disciplined under R2.1, just like any other CPCU, but no evidence suggests that this professor breached his continuing education duty.) If the local CPCU chapter employs an instructor, it may use whatever instructor evaluation criteria and methods it chooses.

The BEI must also determine whether the professor violated his R3.2 duty by allowing "the pursuit of financial gain...to interfere with the exercise of sound professional judgment and skills." As noted in Opinion HCS-107, the BEI will not apply R3.2 to judge the level of compensation a CPCU receives in the marketplace for his or her services Whether the students were unjustly harmed by this professor's conduct cannot be determined based solely on the information given. If the facts supported such a finding, the professor would be informally admonished to cease and desist. If he did not heed the warning, the BEI would reprimand him and recommend his public censure.

CASE HCS-118—Duty of Loyalty to Employer

Bernard Forman, CPCU, assistant manager of a regional office of the Old Line Insurance Company, had been working with one of the casualty department's underwriters to help one of the company's contractor-insureds obtain a sizable government contract. While negotiating insurance costs, Forman disagreed with the underwriter over the amount to charge for coverage. The underwriter believed the account merited a $25,000 annual premium charge, but Bernie thought $2,000 was enough. Bernie told the underwriter that he was making an executive decision to charge only $2,000. The project was awarded to the contractor.

Two months after this experience, the underwriter discovered that Bernie was a silent partner in the agency that handled the contractor's account. He believes that Bernie should remove himself from all further business decisions involving the agency, and has requested the BEI take action. To substantiate the reasonableness of his $2,000 charge, Bernie notes that the job was completed without any losses.

OPINION HCS-118—Duty of Loyalty to Employer

As an employee, Forman has an occupational duty of loyalty to his employer. He cannot discharge that duty unless he is consistently honest about matters that may affect his employer. It therefore follows that Forman's failure to disclose his role as a silent partner is a violation of his R4.1 duty under the Code. However, G4.1 stipulates that the BEI will not hear the matter of an alleged violation of R4.1 until all other remedies have been exhausted. Assuming the employer discovered Forman's failure to disclose his interest in the agency, it may dismiss Forman and/or to take other actions without bringing an ethics complaint to the BEI.

Apart from the employer's decision, the underwriter or any other person could file an ethics complaint that alleged violation of R3.2 and R3.1. Forman may have been motivated by the pursuit of financial gain, but it would be very difficult to prove that he violated his R3.2 duty because the determination of an adequate premium for manuscript coverages leaves ample room for substantial disagreements in judgment.

The BEI believes that Forman's failure to disclose (to his employer) his agency partnership role is an omission of a dishonest or deceitful nature within the meaning of R3.1. Accordingly, the BEI would reprimand Forman and warn him of the more severe penalties that may follow an additional Rule violation.

CASE HCS-119—Expense Accounts and Entertainment Expenses

Gina Finch, CPCU, is a manager of a large branch office of a national insurance company. She often entertains neighbors and friends and charges the expenses to the company. Her expense accounts reflect that she entertained agents. When she wants to show appreciation to office employees, she advises them to entertain friends and show it on their expense accounts as entertaining agents.

Patrick Matthews received permission to take his wife out to dinner and charge it to the company. Because he had reservations about the proposed method of handling personal entertainment expenses, he has written to the BEI to determine whether this sort of conduct would be a breach of the Code.

OPINION HCS-119—Expense Accounts and Entertainment Expenses

The BEI would commend Matthews for observing the spirit of the following G1.2 concept:

> …when a person subject to the Code is uncertain about the ethical propriety of a specific activity or type of conduct, he or she should refrain from engaging in the questionable activity or conduct until the matter has been clarified. Any CPCU or CPCU candidate who needs assistance in interpreting the Code is encouraged to request an advisory opinion from the American Institute's Board of Ethical Inquiry (BEI).

Matthews would be issued an advisory opinion, and it would later be published, with names changed to conceal identities, if appropriate.

R3.3 clarifies that a CPCU will be subject to disciplinary action for the violation of any law or regulation relating to professional activities. The Rule includes violations of Internal Revenue Service (IRS) regulations as well as violations of the Internal Revenue Code (and comparable state laws and regulations).

If Finch and Matthews are complying with the tax laws, and if their employer allows Finch to reward employees with generous expense-account allowances, the BEI sees nothing unethical about the activity of either. Yet, the case suggests that Finch is running afoul of R3.1 by engaging in "any act or omission of a dishonest, deceitful, or fraudulent nature." It appears that she may also be violating the applicable tax laws and regulations. If so, and if a proper complaint were filed, Finch would be reprimanded by the BEI, and harsher penalties considered. Matthews would be warned that his complicity would be considered participating in or condoning a prohibited act within the meaning of R1.2. If he is convicted of a crime, the BEI would immediately suspend his CPCU designation.

CASE HCS-120—Use of CPCU Designation and Key in Advertising

J. R. Smith, CPCU, is an insurance agent in a small town. He starts a promotional campaign that includes a giveaway to clients and potential clients: a pen that reads, "J.R. Smith, CPCU, 25 years as an insurance professional, 1-800-555-5555." Tom Jackson, CPCU, the only other insurance agent in town, writes to the American Institute complaining of Smith's promotional effort. Jackson requests the American Institute to direct Smith to cease and desist. Should Smith be disciplined for violating R8.1?

OPINION HCS-120—Use of CPCU Designation and Key in Advertising

Because R8.1 incorporates by reference the G8.1 Guidelines, the latter have the binding effect of Rules. These Guidelines prevent undignified and unprofessional use of the CPCU designation and key.

Subparagraph a.3 of Guideline G8.1 states that the CPCU designation, initials, and key may not be affixed to any object, product, or property. Smith's use of the CPCU letters on a pen violates this Guideline. Subparagraph e. of this Guideline allows the American Institute to grant exceptions. Any CPCU who contemplates a use of the designation, initials, or key that he or she believes is dignified and professional, but that has not been explicitly authorized, may contact the Ethics Counsel to seek approval. Whenever the BEI finds that a particular use is in violation of the Code, it will first request the violator to cease and desist. Additional penalties will be imposed only if the violator does not comply with the initial request. (Where an unauthorized person is using the designation, the failure to cease and desist will prompt the American Institute to bring legal action.)

CASE HCS-121—Dignity of CPCU in Advertising

A member of the BEI hears a radio advertisement for a CPCU's services that strikes an inappropriately suggestive tone. The BEI member wonders if the CPCU, a leading insurance broker and a part-time teacher of CPCU classes, has allowed his advertising agency to commercialize the designation in an undignified and unprofessional manner. Specifically, does the ad violate the G8.1 Guidelines, which have been incorporated by reference into Rule R8.1 of the Code?

OPINION HCS-121—Dignity of CPCU in Advertising

Although standards and values vary, the BEI cannot acquiesce to the imagination of an advertising agency that compromises the dignity of the CPCU designation. The BEI would request the CPCU to cease and desist and forward a copy of the G8.1 Guidelines to him.

CASE HCS-122—Conflict of Interest

A CPCU agent who is a member of the Board of Directors for the local Boys and Girls Club designs the club's insurance coverage (with other board members' assistance) and places the coverage with one of the insurers she represents. The club directs other interested agents to contact the CPCU agent at her office for information regarding the insurance bid. It also instructs other agencies to provide the quotation directly to the CPCU agent.

Does this constitute a violation of Canons 1 through 9? Would your opinion change if the CPCU agent were merely a club member and not in a position of authority?

OPINION HCS-122—Conflict of Interest

While the case seems to imply it, it does not state whether the CPCU agent has collected her commission on the coverage placed with one of her insurers. If so, the facts represent a conflict of interest that faces the agent. Several provisions of the Code apply, including the following:

- Under R3.1 and R3.2 of the Rules and G1.2 of the Guidelines, she must be certain that designing the coverage for the club and placing it with one of the carriers she represents do not create even the appearance of impropriety or of allowing the pursuit of personal benefit to interfere with the exercise of sound professional judgment.

- Guideline G3.2 provides that the CPCU should not, to the detriment of the insuring public, engage in any business practice or activity designed to restrict fair competition.

- Guideline G3.3 states that the CPCU should not perform professional services under circumstances that would impair her free and complete exercise of sound professional judgment.

- Guideline G6.5 requires the CPCU to keep fully informed on legal limitations imposed upon the scope of professional activities.

This suggests that the CPCU agent, as a director, must at all times act in such a manner that the club's interests are preferred over her own. Furthermore, being in the position of at least potentially benefiting from the placement of the coverage at the expense of the club to which she owes complete loyalty, she must be careful not to violate certain common-law and statutory duties pertaining to directors of corporations, thereby also becoming guilty of breaching R3.3.

The agent can avoid the danger of improper action arising out of the conflict of interest by taking the following steps:

- Fully disclose to the club the amount of commission and other compensation she or her firm receives for placing the Club's coverage.

- Disqualify herself from voting on or influencing the decision-making process of the club in any manner that has a bearing on her or her firm's business interest.

If the facts are changed so that the agent is not in a decision-making position for the club, the key criterion of the conflict of interest, namely the ability to direct business to her own agency, would not exist. Assuming that ordinary club membership would have no bearing on the placement of the club's insurance business, then the indicated provisions of the Code would most likely not apply to the agent.

The CPCU Society's Code of Ethics

This chapter contains the CPCU Society's Code of Ethics as it appeared after the Society's Board of Governors approved the most recent amendments to it in 2005. The Society's Code of Ethics is in Section 4 of its bylaws, as follows:

The Board of Governors, by affirmative vote of two-thirds of its voting members, after following due process procedures adopted by the Board of Governors, shall have the authority to expel, suspend, censure, or reprimand any member for conduct in violation of the ethics standards of the Society as established by the Board of Governors, or for conduct in violation of the CPCU Professional Commitment.

SECTION 4.   It may be a basis for disciplinary action to commit any of the following acts:

a. Specified Unethical Practices

   (1) To violate any law or regulation duly enacted by any governmental body whose authority has been established by law

   (2) To willfully misrepresent or conceal a material fact in insurance and risk management business dealings in violation of a duty or an obligation

   (3) To breach the confidential relationship that a member has with his or her client or with his or her principal

   (4) To willfully misrepresent the nature or significance of the CPCU designation

   (5) To write, speak, or act in such a way as to lead another to reasonably believe that the member is officially representing the Society or a chapter of the Society unless the member has been duly authorized to do so

   (6) To aid and abet in the performance of any unethical practice proscribed under this Section

   (7) To engage in conduct that has been the subject of a presidential or Board of Governors directive to cease and desist

   (8) To engage in any act of a retaliatory nature against another person reporting or providing evidence of an ethics violation

b. Unspecified Unethical Practices

   (1) A member shall not engage in practices that tend to discredit the Society or the business of insurance and risk management.

   (2) A member shall not fail to use due diligence to ascertain the needs of his or her client or principal and shall not undertake any assignment

if it is apparent that it cannot be performed by him or her in a proper and professional manner.

(3) A member shall not fail to use his or her full knowledge and ability to perform his or her duties to his or her client or principal.

c. Procedure

(1) Inquiry

(a) Upon written, signed request, the president shall cause an inquiry to be made for the purpose of determining whether there is reasonable basis to believe a violation of this Section has taken place. Requests should be directed to the executive vice president at the national headquarters.

(b) Inquiry shall be made by a committee appointed by the president. A committee of inquiry (thereafter the "committee") shall be comprised of at least three persons, each of whom shall be a member of the Society. A finding concurred in by the majority of the committees shall be the finding of the committee.

(c) The committee shall review the written request. If the committee finds that the written request does not state allegations that, if sustained, would constitute a violation of this Section, it shall so notify the president, who shall notify the originator of the request. If the committee finds that the written request does state allegations that, if sustained, would constitute a violation of this Section, it may make inquiries of the member whose conduct is the subject of the request, and may make inquiries of other persons who may have knowledge of pertinent facts and circumstances.

(d) On the basis of these inquiries, the committee shall find whether there is or is not sufficient evidence to support the allegations in the request, and shall so notify the president, who shall notify the member whose conduct is the subject of the request, and the originator of the request.

(e) The committee may request guidance and advice from the Board of Governors or from the Ethics Committee. Such opinion or advice shall be reduced to writing and appended to the findings of the committee.

(f) Relevant information gathered by the committee shall be given to any appropriate conference panel.

(2) Conference

(a) Within thirty days after receipt of a committee finding that a violation may have occurred, the president shall appoint a conference panel (hereafter the "panel"), which shall determine whether the conduct described in the request constitutes unethical conduct. The panel shall be comprised of three members of the Society, at least one of whom shall be a member or past member of the Board of Governors and none of whom shall have served on the committee.

(b) Within ten working days after appointment, the panel shall send notice of the purported violation by certified mail, return receipt requested, to the last known address of the member whose conduct is the subject of the request.

(c) The notice shall specify the conduct that is the subject of the request and the specified unethical practice involved and/or that the conduct appears to constitute unspecified unethical conduct, and shall set a time and place for a conference whose time shall be not less than 30 nor more than 90 days from the date of notice and whose place shall be not more than 100 miles from the residence of the member whose conduct is the subject of the request.

(d) At the time and place fixed for the conference, the member whose conduct is the subject of the request shall have an opportunity to be heard, to present witnesses, to question witnesses, and to present written evidence.

(e) Within ten working days after conclusion of the conference, the panel shall issue its finding. The finding of the panel shall be based exclusively on matters presented at the conference. A finding that the conduct is unethical must be a unanimous finding of the panel and shall be in writing.

(f) The panel finding shall be immediately communicated to the president, to the member whose conduct is the subject of the request, and to the originator of the request. In the case of a finding of specified unethical conduct, the panel shall submit its recommendation for action by the Board of Governors through the president.

(g) Where the time limits or the place for the conference called for in these procedures cannot reasonably accommodate the interests of the persons involved or for other good cause, the conference panel may adopt alternative time limits and processes to administer these procedures.

(3) Action

(a) The president shall immediately review the finding of the panel and, in the case of a finding of unspecified unethical conduct, shall direct the member to cease and desist from the unethical conduct. In the case of specified unethical conduct, the Board of Governors shall consider the gravity of the offense and shall expel, suspend, censure, or reprimand the member, and shall direct the member to cease and desist from the unethical conduct. The action of the Board of Governors shall immediately be communicated to the member by certified mail, return receipt requested, at his or her residence.

(b) Expulsion, suspension, or censure of a member shall be reported in the *CPCU News*. Reprimand of a member shall not be reported, and shall be communicated only to the member whose conduct has been found to be unethical.

(c) The Board of Governors shall have prepared a synopsis of each case, without names, resulting in disciplinary action, and shall publish these synopses in *CPCU News* for the education and guidance of all members.

Index